RY

More Praise f

"The moment I began reading *Shame Off You*, I found myself underlining one sentence after another, marveling at the insight and wisdom I found on each page. Denise Pass understands the power of shame not only because she has lived it but also because she has overcome it through the power of the Holy Spirit. Drawing from her poignant and often painful life experiences, along with stories of biblical characters who also struggled with guilt and shame, Denise points us toward the peace we all long for and the freedom we all need. The words of Paul in Romans 8:1—"Therefore, there is now no condemnation for those who are in Christ Jesus"—resound through each chapter, as we sense the weight of shame lifting off our shoulders and the mantle of God's grace taking its place. A heartfelt and powerful work." —**LIZ CURTIS HIGGS**, bestselling author of *Bad Girls of the Bible*

"When it comes to the dance of shame and grace, we are in a constant battle to choose who will lead. In her raw and transparent book *Shame Off You*, Denise shares how, at several points in her life, she could have easily (and expectedly) chosen the path of shame and condemnation. But with God (don't you just love the words 'but with God'?) she fought not just for grace but for restoration and healing for herself and the next generation. Denise's very personal story is a roadmap for living beyond, and recovering from, devastating shame in every area of our lives." —**KATHI LIPP**, bestselling author of *The Husband Project*, *Clutter Free*, and *Overwhelmed*

"*Shame Off You* is a book of healing—with memoir, Scriptural engagement, and encouragement permeating its hope-filled message. If you've ever suffered through the debilitating clutches of shame, you'll find respite, practical help, and authenticity in its pages. Denise Pass's love for Jesus shines through on every single page, and her heart to empower you to let go of shame is contagious in the best possible way." —**MARY DEMUTH**, author of *The Seven Deadly Friendships*

"People get trapped and stuck because of many things in life. Shame is one of them. We've all felt shame before. How we let it define us is our choice. Denise is straightforward in sharing her experience and how God has redeemed and restored her and her family to their true identity in Christ. The good news is that I get to see that played and lived out every Sunday as she leads our people in worship." —**RANDY ORNDORFF**, Lead Pastor, Culpeper UMC, Culpeper, VA

"In *Shame Off You*, Denise gracefully leads us to find the root of shame in our lives whether it be from our own weakness or someone else's. She guides the reader through a simple method of finding the shame-free life. It's a life of freedom that we all desire!" —MICAH MADDOX, author of *Anchored In*

"In *Shame Off You* Denise Pass gives a new hope to any who have experienced the different facets of shame. As a pastor, I am looking forward to using this book in my ministry and I think it will change many lives and help women break free from the stronghold of shame." —JESSIE SQUIRES COLWELL, Lead Pastor, Rappahannock UMC, Flint Hill, VA

"From the feelings of inferiority we experience in day-to-day life to the intense trauma that wants to stay hidden in darkness, Pass offers a candid and much-needed perspective on how God's truth and grace can lift us out of the shadows and set us free from our shame." —DR. FRED MILACCI, Professor and Qualitative Research Consultant, Graduate School of Education, Liberty University, Lynchburg, VA

"This book is an excellent and exhaustive study and warfare manual to confront, combat, and overcome shame. Denise Pass's unique talent and insight help the reader apply biblical principles at every turn in the realm of shame and self-conscience condemnation. Some of the most challenging spiritual battles we face concerning shame are exposed as winnable in every instance. Denise employs real-world experiences and examples to amplify the application of biblical truth and follows up with 'reflective self-assessment' applications with each chapter. This is a must-read for those who want to know how to overcome shame and learn the secret of Shame Off You." —DICK SHERWOOD, Chairman, National School Project

"Denise Pass shares the real life story of her journey from heartache, hurting, and shame to healing, redemption, and hope—hope reinvented and restored. She shares biblical truth and practical principles that will help you put Shame OFF You (instead of shame on you!). I cried and laughed; my heart broke for her and rejoiced with her. In *Shame Off You* you will read a message of grace and forgiveness, freedom and fun, humor and humility, and hope and healing. I couldn't put the book down. Neither will you. Read it and be blessed!" —JEFF ROGERS, Founder and Chairman, Stewardship Legacy Coaching, LLC; author of *Create a Thriving Family Legacy*

"This book deals with a subject not often touched on in the church, that being SHAME. The book is an intense study on hurts that run deep, healing that runs deeper, and the restoring power of Christ. I found it riveting and convicting. We must take our hurts and shame to the Lord. A must read!" —GENE SCHMIDT, Chairman CSMI, VP Hand of Help Ministries

Shame Off You

from Hiding to Healing
• • • • •
Denise Pass

Abingdon Press
Nashville

SHAME OFF YOU
FROM HIDING TO HEALING

Copyright © 2018 by Abingdon Press

All rights reserved.

Library of Congress Cataloging-in-Publication Data has been requested.

ISBN 978-1-5018-6968-6

18 19 20 21 22 23 24 25—10 9 8 7 6 5 4 3 2 1
MANUFACTURED IN THE UNITED STATES OF AMERICA

Contents

Contents

Acknowledgments

I am overcome with gratitude that I got to write this book. It further set me free from shame on a whole new level, and the communion with Christ during the writing of it was life-altering as well.

To my sweet Savior, who showed me how to dissolve shame in my life and replace it with unending joy and peace, I pray You are honored in this work.

To my darling husband, my "Bo," who exemplifies what it means to rise above shame. Through you, I finally know what it feels like to truly be loved and cherished. I love you. Thank you for not just bearing the late nights and early mornings but also encouraging me throughout and being my biggest fan.

To my precious children, who did not get the same level of attention they were accustomed to while I wrote *Shame Off You*, thank you for being my raving cheerleaders and for listening to me as I read excerpts to you "one more time." You and Dad are my heroes and inspiration.

To my mom, DiAnne, who was there in my most horrific moments of shame, catching my tears and pointing me to Christ, I am eternally grateful.

To my dad, Dorse, who did not judge me when I was broken but came alongside and encouraged me to press on, thank you.

Acknowledgments

To my dear friends Erin and Jessie, who rooted me on to write this work, thank you for believing in me and the calling of God on my life.

To Jeff Rogers, who mentored and encouraged me to write, thank you for fanning into flame the gift of God.

To the reader, whatever shame you have encountered in this life, may you know how precious you are in the eyes of God and understand the freedom He has called you to, so you may rise above shame and live in victory. I pray this book can serve as an encouragement and manual to help you time and again when shame tries to snuff out joy. You are loved deeply by Your Creator and He is *for* you.

You Are Not Alone

My family tells me that, as a little girl, I was fascinated with balloons. I liked them so much that I actually ate one. I will spare you the details of where that balloon went. I wanted to soar like a balloon, to be free. I imagined myself like the balloon, rising above my circumstances, no longer held down in this life. But eating a balloon did not make me float away. It only made me feel sick.

Sometimes we desire to escape, we think we can achieve deliverance on our own. We try to fill the void we feel in our souls with anything to help us rise above our circumstances. Like a solitary balloon floating high into the sky, we try to find space free from condemnation. Filling ourselves with our shame coping mechanisms, we think we are making progress. But it is when the Holy Spirit fills us that we truly find our freedom.

We're only human. It's our weakness—and our strength. Together we'll talk about the mistakes we make and the shame we sometimes feel, and together we'll learn the truth, humility, and grace way of approaching Shame Off You. We might even learn to laugh at ourselves in the midst.

What shame fills your balloon? As God reveals areas of shame in our lives in each chapter, let's take a minute to release shame's hold on us. Look for the balloon icon at the end of each chapter and consider the revealed shame you are giving to God. Give it a name and let it go! Then turn to the devotional for more encouragement.

You are not alone. As we begin this journey of kicking shame to the curb, I want to invite you into a family that accepts you—shame and all. You don't have to go it alone. Come explore your new Shame-Off-You life and join the community in a website created just for you at www.shameoffyou.life or hang out with us on Facebook: www.facebook.com/groups/shameoffyou to see what God is doing with the removal of shame in people's lives. You'll find quizzes, tips, and other folks with whom to share victories and failures together—and overcome the cycle and reach of shame in your life.

Part One

Shame's Foundation

CHAPTER ONE

Shame Is Born

A Story of a Girl Who Shrunk Her Shame

Fear not; you will no longer live in shame. Don't be afraid; there is no more disgrace for you. You will no longer remember the shame of your youth and the sorrows of widowhood. —Isaiah 54:4

But healing hurts. To get to the source of our pain, we have to clean the wound, it turns out, with lots of tears—salty ones that sting but begin the cure for our souls when they are offered to our great God and counted by our Lord.
—*Denise*

Pulling my stringy, thinning hair to hide my face, I tried to conceal the fact that I was weeping profusely. Heaving and trying to silence my sobs, I was keenly aware of the gaze of onlookers. Hardly anyone knew me there. I'd felt safe to let down my guard, but to be so broken in front of strangers was not how I wanted my first Sunday at the new church to go. How did I get here? My life felt like a dream, or rather like a nightmare. I tried to remain composed, though my world was completely turned upside down and I just could not hide it anymore. And there I was, like a dam breached, unable to control the emotions I had held in for so long. I was rocking and weeping uncontrollably, and the more I tried to suppress it, the worse it got.

I had purposed in my heart that my children and I would show up full of joy, our shattered lives disguised. But there it was. Shame. It followed me everywhere I went and filled my being and my soul. I couldn't escape it. I couldn't hide it. Imprisoned by its grip, I felt boxed in by the opinions and curious stares of others, real or imagined. Why was I in church with five kids and no husband? Why did our vehicle look like it had been pulled from a scrap yard? Why was I weeping...in public?

Many Rivers to Cross, Many Tears to Shed

For two years, I'd been carrying a burden of shame, ever since the night my (then) husband, when confronted, admitted to having sexually abused one of our children, though he did not give it that name. The shock of this revelation consumed my children and me—it did not seem possible. I felt that the elders at the church we attended then wanted me to keep silent and hide the event, to reconcile with my estranged husband in spite of the explicit danger to our beautiful children. What was explained as being one event we would later find out was not. Every Sunday I answered the altar call, weeping, while the church elders seemed to sweep our greatest sorrow underneath the carpet. It was too much to bear: the shame, the awkward stares of pity and judgment, the constant pressure to reconcile, and the deafening silence that spoke volumes.

The night of the offense, I had woken up in the middle of the night to write a song. The Lord would often inspire songs in my heart in the wee hours of the morning, so this was a somewhat normal occurrence. But that night was different. As I wrote the song, "Draw Me Near," I felt a presence of evil enveloping our home. With fear, I penned lyrics of someone's sorrows and their need to draw near to God. Sometimes when I wrote songs, they were prayers for people I did not know. I thought this must be the case this time, too. Only this time, this song, which spoke of someone's life being turned upside down, was about to become my story. Two hours later, after I finished writing the song, I went to bed.

The next morning, the sun came through the window and a whisper awoke my soul. "Tell your husband that God says you have something to tell me." My husband was in the shower, but I felt a pressing need to go ask this question the Lord had placed upon my heart. I walked into the bathroom and said, "The Lord says you have something to tell me." Silence.

"I'll tell you later. I'm not going to tell you now." My heart was heavy. Instinctively I knew something was wrong, but I did not know what. The day of the beginning of the revelation of sexual abuse in our home, the children and I had to bring a bug to the gastroenterologist. (Only my life!) One of my daughters had been ill for most of her life with celiac disease and now we suspected a parasite as well. I had found this massive creature in our washing machine and the doctor told me to bring it in. Next on the agenda that day was to sing at a nursing home with my home educational co-op. The children were to present the gospel through skits and song. But as I was driving to the doctor's office, the Lord was preparing my heart. Something was wrong. This day would be a defining moment for our family that I could never have imagined. But I guess that is how such times occur. We can be lulled into a sense of thinking we are above crises. It always happens to someone else, right? Wrong. So wrong.

As we drove to the nursing home, the Lord whispered to my heart again. "Ask her how she slept last night." Oh God, no. No. Please no. Not in my family. Choking back the pressure mounting in the back of my throat, I asked one of my daughters, "How did you sleep last night?"

"Not so well. In the middle of the night, Daddy came into my bed and hugged me for a couple of hours."

Silence. All of the children were in the car. Lord, please help me. I can't breathe. What has happened? In as normal a voice as I could muster with a van load of children, I said, "That's strange. We will talk about this later, OK? Are you OK, honey?"

"Yes, mom. Just tired."

As we arrived at the nursing home, I felt as if I was not there. Numb. How was I going to pull myself together to do this presentation with the children? What was my daughter feeling and going through in that moment? I have never had an out-of-body experience, but this day would have been as close as I have ever been to one. It was as if I was watching myself and I somehow was functioning, going through the motions. Looking at my daughter across the room, I saw myself at a similar age. I had made myself a promise that what I encountered when I was twelve would not happen to her. I had been sexually abused, and I wanted to do everything I could to prevent the same thing from happening to my daughters. I surveyed the room and wondered if I was really awake—if this was really happening. Like the puzzle the little girl at my feet was trying to put together, my heart was broken into pieces on the floor. I struggled to breathe and wondered how the pieces of our lives would ever fit back together again. Fighting back tears, I tried to hold on to hope that maybe, just maybe, what my daughter said was different from what my heart was telling me.

Heading back home, I went straight to my husband's office. He worked from home and I home educated, so we were both home a lot. "You need to tell me what you did," I said. "God is revealing things to me. What did you do?"

"I will tell you later" was the response. He had work to do and told me he could not talk.

We had a life group (small group) we had been involved with, though we were supposed to try out a new life group that night. I called the wife of our former small group and told her that I believed my husband had done something wrong but that he wouldn't talk with me about it. "Your husband has already called my husband and they are supposed to meet tonight," she said.

Then there was my sweet girl. I needed to talk with her in a way that would not upset her. As she and I spoke, shame silenced her. "What happened last night, honey?" She awkwardly tried to describe what happened. She knew something was wrong but did not know how to talk about it. Later she would tell me that she did not want to tell me for fear that it would break our family apart. I hugged her and told her that everything was going to be all right. God was going to help us.

That day was a busy one—one event after another—and it was just beginning. Arriving at the home of our new small group, I could not hide my tears. The heaviness in my heart sucked any possibility of a smile. I would go back and forth to the bathroom, splash water on my face, and come back out. When my husband arrived, he was his normal gregarious self. I could not fake it—I've never had a good poker face, and surely not that day. Suddenly everyone left the room and it was just the two of us on the couch. I looked over at him and said, "I know what you did, and I know you are going to our old small group to talk with the leader tonight." Stunned silence. "The Lord is revealing it to me. Just tell me what you did."

"I will tell you when I get in the car," he said. I was trying to put the pieces of this horrific puzzle together, but he was avoiding me. I had already made plans to stay with a friend that night.

"The children and I are not going home tonight. We are not coming home until you tell me everything you have done," I said, then burst into tears. We never allowed the children to go on sleepovers out of a desire to protect them. The irony that the danger was in my own home was too painful to consider. As we left the home of the new small group, I called him. "OK. You are now in your car. Tell me what you have done."

> Shame threatened to stifle our existence. Shame that such sin was in our camp. Christians.

He laughed. "I'm not going to tell you now." There are few moments in my life where I have felt the way I did that night. When all you thought you knew, you realize you didn't. The agony of the revelation that you have been living a lie is too painful to put into words. But that night I knew everything was going to be different. Several hours later, the phone rang. "I need to talk with you. Can you meet?"

"No, I will not meet with you until I know what you have done,"

I answered. "You can tell me on the phone." The words that came out of his mouth pierced my soul and were too much for me to take in. I cannot even write them here. Nonsensical and offensive rationalization of what he had done. I never would have imagined words like that coming from someone who had vowed to love and protect me. Never could I have thought such words could come from a father. But they did. And the pain was too much to bear. My girl, my precious sweet daughter, who already had too much to bear with celiac disease, was now burdened with this. Oh, God, why?

She was thirteen years old, and in the midst of other agonizing revelations that would follow, the events of that horrific night would be minimized, adding further trauma. Her father had assumed that she did not understand what was happening or that she was asleep when he came into her bedroom. This heaped further shame on us. And my precious girl? She wasn't asleep. She pretended to be. She just waited what seemed like an eternity for him to leave. That's what shame did that night—it silenced a victim who was filled with confusion that someone who claimed to love her would ever do something to harm her. Not her daddy.

The church had counseled my husband to contact social services the next morning to confess. He then left our home. Nothing could have prepared me for the horrors we would encounter in the revelation of sexual abuse, the debilitating recovery from the abuse, the walk through an agonizing divorce, and the family and criminal court processes that would drag out over the next five years. Nothing. Overwhelmed with a sudden flurry of court dates and meetings, I did the best I could to try and comprehend all that was happening. Fear and worry enveloped me. But as my children and I looked to a Christmas alone, for the first time in a long time, oddly, we felt free.

My husband had been very controlling, and after living in that environment for a long time, we were surprised and even felt a little guilty that there was relief mingled with our intense grief. The excruciating heaviness in our hearts could not be lifted, but there with the biggest sorrow of our lives was this thing we did not expect—freedom. My husband had never allowed us to have a dog. "Let's go buy a puppy," I told the kids. They were thrilled. In that moment, we felt a little joy. There was this sweet little puppy. Who was not housebroken. What was I thinking?

Then there was my oldest boy. He had always wanted to play sports, but my husband disapproved—said it was too much like the pursuit of the American dream, too worldly. We needed to stay home. Well, not anymore. I signed my boy up for baseball and myself for the gym. We went to our first movie. We went on field trips together. We got cable in our home. We. Had. Fun. Yes, I probably went off the deep end. OK, I did. But sometimes part of the healing process is exploring new boundaries, and we can go to extremes while we adjust to our new normal. The moments of fun we enjoyed together became a respite and a source of hope in the midst of the most agonizing moments of our lives, but it was temporary. Our new normal was not easy. We were "that" home. You know, the people already on the fringe with home education now had an additional stigma to bear: the father of the home was gone. Rumors about the cause were everywhere in our tight-knit homeschool and church communities. Was he unfaithful? Was I? Had he harmed the children? Were we getting divorced? Our pursuit of finding joy was also admittedly an escape from the constant shame that surrounded us. People would talk with my estranged husband and then be against me. Wherever we went there were reminders. Events. Places. People. All wondering what had happened to our family. And then there was the pervasive court process and the reality that my husband did not recognize the gravity of what he had done. We were supposed to just forgive and move on, but my heart and my children's hearts were devastated. I was cast in a negative light for keeping the children from their father. I felt blame for protecting my children. *Shame on me.* The court had imposed supervised visitation. The children did not want to be forced to see their father, and some in the community thought my children's wishes didn't matter.

My children felt the shame deeply. And the original traumatic episode was only the tip of the iceberg. More painful revelations to come would pierce all of our hearts. Shame threatened to stifle our existence. Shame that such sin was in our camp. Christians. There in the midst of our struggle with shame was constant pressure from many different places.

A people pleaser by nature, I felt like such a sinner when I went against the counsel of church leaders. In our multiple meetings, I felt as though I was being instructed about how I should handle our predicament. I was told that I would be in sin to get a divorce since what my husband did was not "adultery" because it was not with an adult. Really? "What about Matthew 5:32?" I asked. "'But I say to you that everyone who divorces his wife, except on the ground of sexual immorality, makes her commit adultery' [ESV]. The word for sexual immorality is *pornea*. That is any and all sexual immorality." They still encouraged me to let my estranged husband come to church with us. Church. The one place we could come and worship God became a place of pressure, too. Oh, and shame, too.

On another occasion, a well-meaning leader pointedly asked me if I thought I could hear God above the leaders hearing from

God for me. You betcha. Never had I been more grateful to know the truth in God's word than when shamed for thinking for myself. Already in the pit of shame, I was at an all-time low. Evidently, I was not even a good Christian now. *Shame on me.* Who was it that got us into all this mess? My husband. The one who the leaders met with weekly, who the leaders were going to allow to live on the church campus in an RV while he waited for me to reconcile with him. But what about the victims? Did they have a say? Or were they going to be shamed until they acquiesced? What about the sheer terror we felt, knowing that just because someone was caught did not mean we were safe. Did we matter? By the grace of God alone, the Lord strengthened me and enabled me to get out of that church and to make a new life for my children and me. But, even still, I had to struggle through self-righteous pleas trying to shame and condemn us (control us). No words can adequately express the pain of having the tables flipped on you when you are barely making it as a mom experiencing the greatest grief of your life. The pain I felt for my children would serve as strength to fight for them—even if

It is in crying out to God from our place of shame that we obtain victory.

I was blamed and shamed. Proverbs 31:8 pushed me on: "Speak up for those who cannot speak for themselves; ensure justice for those being crushed."

I had been building a career as a songwriter and worship leader, so when I received an offer to serve on a worship team from another church, I loaded up my broken children and left my former church. A month after we left, I received a phone call from one of the leaders of the church we had

left. "We want you to know that you are not in sin to get a divorce."
While I was grateful for that call, I knew God had already released
me through His Word from the shame I felt from that church, but
the scars were deep. Stepping away from what we knew into a new
situation was not easy, but for my children and me, it was once
again freedom. The legal drama would continue to inflict damage
for several years, but for now, I thought we were safe. I thought we
would heal. But healing hurts. To get to the source of our pain, we
have to clean the wound, it turns out, with lots of tears—salty ones
that sting but begin the cure for our souls when they are offered to
our great God and counted by our Lord.

Showing up on that Sunday morning at the new church was a
triumph, though it felt so hard. Was I making a mistake? Would we
be accepted here, or shamed once again? Silenced and ostracized
by my hidden shame, I had felt so bold leaving my former church
in the wake of an enormous heartbreaking scandal, but now, I
could not compose myself. Shame found me there, too. I couldn't
escape it.

That first day at the new church they had arranged to do
cardboard testimonies. One by one, congregants walked across the
stage that day, holding out their cardboard signs in a silent declaration
of what they were before Christ and on the flip side, what God had
done for them after salvation. Their life stories, summarized in a few
simple words, were heartrending, their testimonies of God's grace
and power were empowering. And then someone walked across the
stage holding out a sign that said Victim of Sexual Abuse on one
side and Healed and Restored on the other. Could I dare to hope for
recovery from our mess like they seemed to have experienced? Was
victory possible? Could God heal my children and me? I believed in

God. Believed He was all-powerful. But this. It seemed impossible. I did not see the way. As hard as I tried to suppress the tears that were streaming down my face, there was a freedom in finally being able to let it out despite the shame. I did not care anymore. Like the woman reaching for Christ's robe, I was at the end of my proverbial rope. I longed for the healing as shown by that person who had survived sexual abuse and had overcome shame enough to walk across that stage and claim to be healed and restored. I had been victimized by sexual abuse as a child and had healed and moved on, but now, how was I supposed to help my children heal? Could God heal my crushed heart? Could He keep my children's hearts and faith safe? Where was God in all of this?

Giving into uncontrollable weeping that day was a beginning to the healing my heart so desperately needed. Boxing the shame up was not working. Finally stepping out from the shadows of the condemnation that shame placed on me and exposing the deep anguish within was so humbling—and yet so freeing. My deep secret was out. At the other church I felt like I had to have an attitude of strength while I crumbled inside. Here at the new church, I could share my burden, and did, with the pastor. I was out from underneath the control of the other church and my soon-to-be ex-husband. I did not have to pretend to be perfect anymore. I did not have to hold it together anymore. Still, in a heap of sobs, I felt shame compounding with the shame I already felt because I could not control my emotions. I completely gave myself over, anyway, unable to care how pitiful I looked. There I was, a glorious mess over the shame I felt and at the same time committing shame violation number two—crying in public.

Weeping May Last for a Night

What is it about crying that makes us feel shame? We are shamed for being less than perfect, then doubly shamed for crying out for help about it. Sounds like a serious plan of condemnation from the enemy! But what looks like weakness becomes a secret source of strength for those who know and trust in God.

For the record, crying has been given a bad rap. Weeping in cultures all over the world is deemed something to be embarrassed by. Goodness, we even apologize when we do it. Showing emotion is often seen as a sign of weakness, sometimes associated with mental or personality disorders. Add the sting of shame to the feelings of inferiority for just expressing emotions, and the overwhelming humiliation begins to paralyze us and affect our ability to function. Getting to this place of crying out is made even more difficult with the lingering shame for doing so.

> Hiding shame does not heal it; it makes it multiply.

But there is another type of crying. Set aside the helpless, I'm-so-ashamed crying. Instead, there is a sweet place of brokenness where we cry out and look to God for comfort. And it is in crying out to God from our place of shame that we obtain victory. Admitting our need is not a display of weakness, but a testament of relationship. But it can be so very hard to admit that aching need. God made us for relationship, to know Him intimately. We were not made for independence, but dependence upon our loving God. There is no shame in that. When we cry out to God, He helps us to recognize the oppressive presence of shame, so we can rightly deal with this stigmatizing emotion.

In Scripture, Hannah felt the scorn from shame in being childless. She knew all too well the taunts of those around her, especially from a rival wife. She wept at the altar. She was not enough. She could not bear children. And there was nothing she could do about it. This is a classic situation of shame. Circumstances we cannot control, yet we somehow accept the shame as if we earned it. But Hannah had a weapon. She cried out to God—the only One who could truly remove her shame. And God answered. Sometimes we have to wait for the Lord to restore. We may have to walk through shame to be able to appreciate the shame being removed from us. Hannah's tears were counted that day, and the priest serving in the church saw her too:

> Hannah was in deep anguish, crying bitterly as she prayed to the LORD. And she made this vow: "O LORD of Heaven's Armies, if you will look upon my sorrow and answer my prayer and give me a son, then I will give him back to you. He will be yours for his entire lifetime, and as a sign that he has been dedicated to the LORD, his hair will never be cut." As she was praying to the LORD, Eli watched her. Seeing her lips moving but hearing no sound, he thought she had been drinking. "Must you come here drunk?" he demanded. "Throw away your wine!" "Oh no, sir!" she replied. "I haven't been drinking wine or anything stronger. But I am very discouraged, and I was pouring out my heart to the LORD. Don't think I am a wicked woman! For I have been praying out of great anguish and sorrow." "In that case," Eli said, "go in peace! May the God of Israel grant the request you have asked of him." "Oh, thank you, sir!" she exclaimed. Then she went back and began to eat again, and she was no longer sad. (1 Samuel 1:10-18)

There is so much to learn from Hannah when we are surrounded by shame. She did not try to fix her situation. She did not try to cover up her shame. She simply went to the only One who could. And she wept before her great God, surrendering to His will. But she also did something astonishing in her prayer—she was not merely looking for the release of shame. She wanted to honor God for His removal of it. She would give her son back to Him. Our shame never really is about us after all. It might feel like it, but we feel shame until we come before God. Like a magnet, shame draws us either nearer to God or propels us away. Hannah knew where her help truly came from. She clung to God and let go of her shame. She also knew that the one who commands armies—El Shaddai—could surely remove shame off her soul. She demonstrated this by leaving her shame there at the altar. She did not carry it anymore.

There are many such altars every Sunday where people have the bravery to come up out of their seat and lay their burdens and shames down. The very public transparent display of my shame on that altar initially hurt so deeply. Like Hannah, I did not hold back. It led to confessing the secrets hidden within, the very thing I never wanted to mention again. There I shared what I had been prevented from sharing before. And instead of finding shame and pressure, I found acceptance and compassion. Somehow, I had thought concealing my shame would make my own unwanted testimony disappear. Surely the scorn and condemnation I felt would someday be removed. But hiding shame does not heal it; it makes it multiply. Shame takes on many forms in our lives and colors our world with guilt and humiliation. Shame screams out "condemnation" to a weary soul too tired to fight the accusation. It tries to define us, but we can rise above shame. Shame impacts us all, but it is how we deal with shame that determines the lasting impact shame has on our life.

Shame seems insurmountable and hopeless to us when we listen to it. But that's what shame does. It makes it seem like there is no way out. Trapped within the walls of our own mind, we don't even recognize all the shame we are bound by, but we try to combat this shame through our own devices nonetheless. We might not even be cognizant of our own approaches to deal with shame. Maybe we rationalize it or try to ignore it, but underneath we let shame chip away at our worth. We consider and turn the matter over in our mind a million times, trying to cast off the yoke of shame. Perhaps we allow bitterness to overtake us as we seethe at those who hurt us or who are judging us. Self-made strategies and techniques lack sustaining power to remove an entrenched, invisible force such as shame. Nice anecdotes and willpower cannot extinguish it, either. In all our struggling with shame, could it be that God has a better way to remove shame and that He can even use its presence in our lives for good?

Review and Reflection

Let's Recap

Some of life's greatest sorrows also bring us the greatest shame. Boxed in by our pain, we cannot figure a way out. When I was trying to hide shame or even trying to find ways to temporarily escape it, shame still lingered. If shame is not dealt with biblically, it confines and paralyzes us and keeps us from living the abundant life Christ has for us that is shame-free. It was not until I was willing to fully cry out to God that I began to see deliverance of the shame that crushed my soul.

Reflection Questions

1. Have you ever felt shame for something you did not cause? How did you process the shame?
2. Why do we try to hide shame?
3. Can you relate to Hannah in the grief she encountered and shame she felt because she was not able to have what others could?

Name Your Shame—and Let It Go

What is the source of your shame? What is it that you don't even want to utter, lest you feel buried in shame? Sometimes when we are willing to give voice to what is limiting us, we are then able to remove its ability to define us and limit its power in our lives. In each chapter, you will be invited to identify the shame you are feeling. Write it down here and ask God to help you let it go.

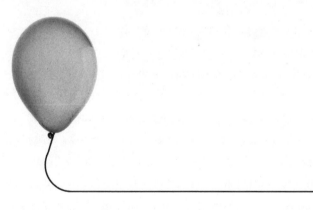

DEVOTIONAL

Disposing of the Shame Arising from Trauma

But the LORD GOD helps me; therefore I have not been disgraced; therefore I have set my face like a flint, and I know that I shall not be put to shame. —Isaiah 50:7 (ESV)

In the wake of the biggest devastation of my life, our home was placed in foreclosure and my children and I moved to a new home in the boonies. Friends thought we were a part of the witness protection program. Even GPS could not find us—and, in a way, we liked it.

When we go through tragic events, we don't want to have the reality of our situation out in the open. It hurts too much. Fear of going out in public and encountering someone who is aware of our shame makes us want to withdraw even further. The problem is, the enemy targets those who are shocked, hurt, and isolated.

When we allow shame to separate us from others, we give it the power to defeat us. Yet God's GPS never fails. He is our ever-present comfort, bringing healing to the deep places. This is the difference between those who depend on God and those who do not. We have hope in sorrow. Peace in turmoil. Those who hope in themselves or in circumstances have temporal hope that ebbs and flows with life's rollercoaster ride.

Reminders of traumatic events trigger our past pain and try to keep us shackled to our former burdens until we learn to approach those memories biblically.

A Prayer

Lord, thank You for meeting us in the most traumatic places of our lives and for healing us. Heal everyone reading this, dear God. Show them that Your love and grace is enough.

CHAPTER TWO

Shame's Condemnation

Exposing and Escaping the Condemnation of Shame in Our Surrounding Culture

> *There is therefore now no condemnation for those who are in Christ Jesus.* —Romans 8:1 (ESV)

> It's the unspoken pains that are often the biggest source of shame. —*Denise*

Looking around the plane, I felt nauseated from the turbulence and the constant noise as a two-year-old boy kept running up and down the aisle, drinking from everyone's cups. Geez. Somebody ought to get that kid in line. Everyone knows the protocol when a poorly behaved kid is making a bold statement of disobedience in public. Shame the parent. That's right. Look at the parent with disdain, because everyone knows their parenting skills are better. Only no one ever thinks to question the reason behind the behavior. That kid? He was my newly adopted son from Russia. He had never been on a plane before, did not speak our language, and running up and down the aisle stopped him from banging his head and screaming. Seemed like a good solution to me at the time. We had to navigate carefully how we managed our new son's behavior, and this was no easy task with the inner ear pressure doing its trick to a little one's ears.

Ever had one of those proud mama moments? When your children have brought upon you a huge dose of shame and you want to disappear? This kind of shame is prideful and focused on self. As a parent I realized that I would be praised when my children were well behaved, but when they weren't, well, let's just say shame knocked loudly on my door. This kind of shame comes from our identity being tied to our position as a parent. But when my identity is as a child of God, then my occupation as a parent changes to one that cares more about lovingly correcting my child for their good, than for my glory.

> Addressing shame opens the door for redemption, where hiding shame just causes it to grow.

We all want to avoid shame, but sometimes shame is a good indicator that we need to examine our hearts. Maybe there is something askew that needs to be addressed. Addressing shame opens the door of possibility for redemption through shame, where hiding shame just causes shame to grow. We can't overcome shame unless we know what we are aiming at. Shame is best defeated when we acknowledge the elephant in the room and address it biblically and lovingly.

Discipline was one of the hardest things I ever had to do as a parent. When a child was caught in a sin, there was a dread in my soul. I knew I had to address the disobedience. To not address it would cause their misbehavior to multiply. God is the same way with us. When we sin, shame gets our attention. God is loving when he deals with our sin, and He wants to reveal and eradicate the cause of the shame. Feelings of shame rising from our sinful choices will not just go away, and our hearts can become hardened when we permit shame to go unchecked. Shame was not meant to distance us from God, but to help us draw nearer by responding to conviction and getting rid of the obstacle in our relationship with God. Staying in the fight against sin and shame in our lives leads us to redemption. We don't have to fear shame. We just need to be able to examine it without being put off by it. Just as I sought to raise my children in the Lord and had to use discipline to help my children understand what was right and wrong, God is our parent and uses conviction to draw us back to Himself. Discerning between condemnation and conviction is imperative for us to be able to hear the voice of God when shame calls our name.

Condemnation Versus Conviction

The most essential thing we can pass on to our children is something we also need: to be attentive to the conviction of the Holy Spirit so much so that the voice of our flesh becomes less. Rising above condemnation is hard. But not impossible. It is far easier to combat sin before it leads to condemnation. If we walk around in condemnation after He has already forgiven us, we live defeated lives. If we defeat the shame from our condemnation by submitting to conviction, we overcome shame and live worthy lives. If we are unresponsive to the conviction of the Holy Spirit, we are distracted once again and live for pleasure, leading unproductive lives that likely cause shame to grow and hinder an intimate walk with God.

Maybe your moments of shame look a lot different than mine. Still, the same raw emotion of attack on our very personhood cuts to the core. Shame knocks on the door of all of our hearts at one time or another. We just might not readily recognize it, but we feel its condemning presence in one form or another. Discerning between condemnation and conviction is critical to the abundant life Christ accomplished. Our own hearts condemn us and make it difficult to apprehend the grace that God gives us when feeling shame. Even if we have not endured a significant traumatic event causing shame, shame can still be hidden within our lives, undetected because of its constant presence all around us, but leaving its fingerprint on our minds nonetheless.

Condemnation

Condemnation does not take into account the grace or forgiveness of God. Condemnation does not fit a Christian and shame can't reach a forgiven soul. Condemnation is only successful if the one condemned believes shame's lie—that we are unforgivable and that our shame is too high for Christ to cover it. Where condemnation is based on our works, not Christ's, conviction is based on relationship.

Conviction

Learning to hear the voice of God and follow it takes some practice. I remember my children each coming to me at different times, grappling with what God was telling them. Was it the voice of God, or just their flesh? Or was it the accuser, trying to throw them into shame? No one can hear God for another person. Our children need to learn to listen to God all on their own. The best preparation for hearing the voice of God is simply getting into God's Word. Establishing habits of seeking God lays the best foundation to be able to recognize the voice of God. We will make mistakes and slip into hyper-spirituality or legalism. It is part of the growth curve. There is no shame in that either. But as we consistently go back to God's Word and ask for wisdom, He promises to give wisdom to all, generously without finding fault.

The Groups We Trust Most Can Be Sources of Condemnation

The pervasiveness of shame makes it something that we all must contend with in one way or another, but we might not readily see the many ways shame manifests itself within our own social groups, in the culture of our families, social relationships, work, or church. We are wired to want acceptance, which is what makes group acceptance so powerful to those with a people-pleasing persona. Maybe you recognize some of these familiar places where shame has been interwoven in your life. But hang on, because help is on the way.

Trauma and the Church

The church is God's agent for recovery to a lost world when life is hard, ministering to people with God's grace and truth and meeting them at their point of spiritual and physical need. A place of refuge that the Holy Spirit uses to convict us of sin and righteousness in our lives so we will draw near to God, the church sometimes has shame lurking in unexpected places. It's the unspoken pains that are often the biggest source of shame. Churches can become a place where shame breeds when we silence victims because we cannot mention what is "shameful." Covering up abuse scandals in churches does not extinguish shame, it makes it flourish. Broken families hide in churches and feel the weight of their status deeply. At the discovery of our new reality, I hoped my church would help me navigate the horrors of our situation. Instead, I felt condemned in my shame as I was called to meetings and felt pressured into reconciliation with my estranged husband, despite the very real danger to my children. My heart was inclined toward reconciliation, but the Spirit warned me that it was not safe. The stigma of our situation was excruciatingly painful and not talking about it made us feel isolated and labeled. I am not suggesting gossip is appropriate, or communicating without discretion, but I felt in the church's desire to encourage reconciliation, the leaders recommended it without knowing the full story.

Exposure brings repentance, but concealment keeps us bound in shame. What begins as trying to provide care for church members can morph into spiritual abuse when leaders step over the boundary line of providing counsel to shaming people with that counsel. The condemnation victims feel grows if they do not follow the counsel of people who mean well but honestly are just not equipped to handle cases of abuse.

Churches can mishandle such cases because of shame; they may want to cover the possibility of such a grievous sin being within the congregation. But churches can overcome the stigma of shame and become a safe place of healing that brings light to traumatic cases of abuse instead of trying to hide them. Even if you have not experienced shame from an abuse scandal, there is another shame that breeds within church walls that needs to be stopped.

Church and "Normal" Shame

You know the drill. The church doors are open. You should be there! And when you get there, you just don't feel like you fit in. And what's that? You are late? Again? And maybe your kid is screaming at the top of his lungs, too. The stares all around you tell you what you are already thinking. You are not a good enough parent. You are a mess. You just can't get your act together. Or maybe someone gossiped about you because they don't like you or the position you hold. Shame upon shame. And this is just scratching the surface. It isn't as if the church is to blame. Its inhabitants are not perfect, after all. But still we try to be so perfect in the church, don't we?

Once we are saved and our outward appearance is cleaned up, we can wrongly turn to religiosity or legalism and attempt to maintain a look of perfection on the outside. We dare not expose the shame of being less than, especially as a Christian. Looking to others for affirmation can become an insidious snare, especially when it plays out at church. Church—a vessel for the grace and acceptance of Christ—can instead be a place of condemnation, when its members forget the forgiveness they were once granted. The irony is that it is in confessing our weaknesses that we find grace and our shame is extinguished. The church has one of the greatest capacities to inflict shame and pain in our lives because we don't expect it from that source. We naively have our rose-tinted

> Family is where we first learn what it means to be known and loved—or not. Family can be a powerful incubator for shame.

glasses on, convincing ourselves that because everyone is a Christian at church, we will be unconditionally accepted and loved. This thinking is flawed on many levels.

First, everyone is not necessarily a Christian because they grace the doorway of a church. Christian culture can imitate true Christianity. All of our efforts to be good people are mere religion and fall short of the salvation that was freely given by the grace of God alone. Those who have accepted this free gift of salvation recognize their need to also abide in this grace. But we, too, even while saved, can still be influenced to walk after the flesh.

Second, various maturity levels within church walls affect how the church body relates to one another. Paul addressed the church at Corinth on this important message concerning the maturity of believers:

> Brothers and sisters, I could not address you as people who live by the Spirit but as people who are still worldly—mere infants in Christ. I gave you milk, not solid food, for you were not yet ready for it. Indeed, you are still not ready. You are still worldly. For since there is jealousy and quarreling among you, are you not worldly? Are you not acting like mere humans? (1 Corinthians 3:1-3 NIV)

Paul was talking to the church, not the world. Walking in the Spirit makes all the difference in the world. The church is composed of sinful people who do not always know how to deal with shame. But we can recognize the maturity level of believers by the fruit in their lives and not receive the shame cast our direction by immature believers.

Third, our expectations can lead us to discouragement. When

we expect acceptance and don't get it, we revert to shame. Something must be wrong with us. Or maybe the church, meant to be a place of healing, can become a place of pain. The good news is that there is a better way.

I've painted a hard picture of the church here, though truly, I love the church. I love it too much not to speak up for the problems within it. Paul spoke about the same issues thousands of years ago. The church is still beautiful and called to represent Christ to a lost world. When the church rises up and helps brothers and sisters remove the mantle of shame, rather than covering its people with shame, God can use the beautiful bride of Christ to help its members be more like Christ. When our expectations are based in the reality of the spiritual battle all around us, we don't let shame condemn others but make a way for our fellow brothers and sisters to escape it. When we maintain humility by seeing our perpetual need for discipleship, we put ourselves in a place to be a recipient of grace, not shame.

Family

Family, the people God has sovereignly placed in our lives to witness life's crazy turns together, can be the most important vessel to shape the level of shame we encounter as we navigate through condemnation and acceptance. Family is where our real identity is displayed. And family is where shame can be born, or where it dies.

The fabric of our lives is filled with both precious and sorrowful moments; where man's heart is transparently shown—the good, the bad, and the ugly. And when sin is woven into that fabric, shame grows. Shame can be evident in small degrees, everything from those blissful moments when your children embarrass you tremendously, or you embarrass them (paybacks). Whether it was children making unpleasant noises or messes in public or exhibiting behavior that caused even grown men to blush, the family is indeed a crucible God uses to shape us and form our character. Family life was never supposed to be neat. But the pressure to have the perfect family can be a massive source of shame for us if we let it be.

Then there is the debilitating shame—from abuse, estrangement, divorce, death—that injures your family and breaks it apart. When our identity is formed in our family, who are we now? Where is our refuge? Shame hisses at us that there is no recovery when tragedy tries to deal a fatal blow to all we knew, but God is in the business of bringing dead things back to life.

We all crave acceptance from others; it is part of the inner desire to be known and celebrated. The family is where we first learn what it means to be known and loved—or not. It can be one of the most powerful incubators for shame. I saw this play out in the adoption of my son.

> When we try to get our worth from our work, we give it power to rule us while we clamber for success.

One morning in the spring of 2004, I woke up suddenly with a sense that the Lord was speaking to me. My son had been born. Somewhere in the world was a little fella that I was going to adopt and be his mama. Some called me crazy; I already had four children. I already had a son. So . . . why? Answer: There was a place of pain in me that remembered the rejection I felt as a kid, and I longed to bring to another child the acceptance I so remembered wanting. If I could help just one.

We adopted him from Russia, and my precious youngest son joined our family when he was two. Soon—through his behavior and struggle to adapt to a foreign environment—we realized he was exhibiting signs of abuse or neglect at the hands of the only family he knew: the orphanage. Banging his head against the wall and screaming incessantly was our new normal. We worked to help him know that we loved him, but it would be years before we began to see the fruit of our efforts and healing for him. Sometimes we can think we are living the perfect family life only to have it shatter in front of our very eyes. There in the midst of an incredible story of redemption was the unraveling of all I thought I knew—and shame grew.

Maybe it is your family where you encountered shame and maybe you did not recognize it because it was built into your culture. As a little girl, I felt like I had no voice. When I would speak up, I was quickly silenced and felt like my opinion did not matter. This, too, was shame. And this feeling of inferiority was pressed upon me like a label, so hard to remove. If I felt "less than" in the culture of my own home, what would I feel like in the world?

Maybe the place you hoped would be a place of refuge became a place of pain instead. When you wanted comfort, you were silenced in shame. When you sought acceptance, you felt rejection. Maybe there was a culture of sin infiltrating the family unit that was handed down from generation to generation. No one knew how to eradicate it and dared not speak about it or against it. It was shameful to do so. Or maybe it was all you ever knew. Perhaps it was hidden, unspoken because no one recognized the dysfunction, or they were fearful to speak out against it. Shame cripples families because we dare not speak against each other. Families can perpetuate shame in our lives instead of setting us free when we don't love the people nearest to us enough to share the truth that sets them free. Keeping shame hidden and enabling others to avoid consequences is not love, after all. But loving one another enough to expose sin in a redemptive manner so repentance and restoration can take place is what makes conviction so beautiful, and the opposite of the fruit of guilt and shame that condemnation brings.

Parents can use shame to coerce their children into obedience, or children can use shame to manipulate their parents by reminding them of their failures, too. We see this played out in grocery stores everywhere, every day. Parents desperate to control their children's behavior try to shame their children into obedience. Children just learn to exist in the shame culture or overthrow it eventually. Correction is a useful tool in the parent/child relationship, but when shame is mingled, the message can wound deeply. Siblings can join the shame cycle they see within the family framework and use shame to control others by using past failures to humiliate or minimize one another by criticizing supposed weaknesses or inferiorities seen in one another. There is a better way.

Families can admit their flaws in a safe place when the Word of God is at the center of the family culture and all recognize their own unique deficiencies. Rather than avoiding topics because of shame, we learn to face them without condemnation and expose the shame in a redeeming way rather than just ridiculing the flaws of the people around us. When we expect to be a flawed people, we embrace grace and let go of shame. There is a beautiful freedom that comes from knowing ourselves and being OK with our imperfections and surrounding ourselves with people who root for us rather than mock us in our weaknesses.

Work

The television show *The Office* was and still is widely popular, likely due to how much people felt they could relate to the dysfunctional behavior—the tedium, the head games, the shame dealt out by bosses and coworkers alike—exhibited in the episodes. I can relate, too. Once when I was working for the Department of Justice many years ago, I inadvertently sent the wrong document from my Wang computer to the head secretary, who, in turn, sent that document out to all the Department of Justice offices across the United States of America. True story. It was supposed to be a funeral announcement. It may as well have been. I had sent my résumé instead. The laughter ringing in those halls lasted for weeks. And I did not need to wear blush for a while, either. For those of you who do not know what a Wang is, I feel no shame for my age. I wrote the book on removing shame, after all.

Maybe the workplace is a place of scorn or shame for you. Coworkers make your vocation a place of misery as you encounter their snide remarks or perhaps even worse: their silence. Snubs and bantering intended to elevate one person over another and politics or power plays are really attempts to use shame to belittle others to promote self. Again, there is a better way.

When we try to get our worth from our work, we give power to our work environment to rule us while we clamber for success. And when our drive for success is dampened by shame from failures or the work culture in general, we can only overcome and persevere by remembering a higher motivation. The motivation for our work cannot come from other people. People are fallible and their ever-changing opinion would have us enslaved to shame. Paul reminded believers just who they were truly working for and why as he spoke to the church at Colossae, "Whatever you do, work at it with all your heart, as working for the Lord, not for human masters, since you know that you will receive an inheritance from the Lord as a reward. It is the Lord Christ you are serving" (Colossians 3:23-24 NIV).

When our work and lives are truly focused on serving the Audience of One, we don't fear shame or seek accolades, we want just His glory alone. We don't worry about promotion from man, because our eternal reward lasts much longer, and man's approval or disapproval no longer holds the power it once did.

Relationships

If God who knows everything does not condemn us, why do we? Is there a way out of the shame game that lasts? In all of these scenarios of church, family, and work, shame can be used as a tool to control or harm. In relationships within all of these spaces, shame can manifest itself as manipulation and guilt trips and morph into abuse. We can become so accustomed to the culture of shame in our relationships that we don't see the underlying causes, but we feel its presence nonetheless. People are controlled and controlling others moment by moment with shame. Desperate to cover our flaws, we try to cover or escape our shame. The consequences can be deadly when people feel so shamed they despair of life. But there is another source of shame we might not see so readily.

Condemnation Is a Head Game and We Do It to Ourselves

Ah...the battle of the mind. More battles take place in the mind on a daily basis than we could ever count. It is estimated that we have between sixty thousand and seventy thousand thoughts in a given day. How many of those thoughts are focused on some form of shame? Who can tell? It might be as simple as a thought like, *I should have done this or that* or *I should not have eaten that* or *My house is a mess* or *I am a failure* or *No one likes me*, and the list goes on and on. Although the flood of thoughts and ideas is intimidating, we can take captive those thoughts that are shameful. *If* we recognize them.

When the source of shame is our own thoughts, we can ask God to help us recognize the thought patterns that are condemning us so we can begin to do the work of redeeming our mind. Like these:

Self-Worth

Shame has a way of making us feel inferior. We bear a label that hurts too much to wear. Self-worth can then become performance-based as we try to remove our invisible label. We seek to convince our souls that we are enough, based on our achievements. The only problem is, when we fall short of goals of who we think we are supposed to be or what we think we were supposed to have accomplished, our worth takes a nose-dive. There is a better way.

In Christ, our worth could never be based on performance because Christ alone defines our worth. With His blood, He covered every single transgression and communicated to our souls that His love was so great for us that He would die on our behalf. Christ is our worth. We who are in Christ no longer live, so how could shame impact us so greatly? Paul, too, revealed this to the Galatian church that this identity of ours is in Christ alone: "My old self has been crucified with Christ. It is no longer I who live, but Christ lives in me. So I live in this earthly body by trusting in the Son of God, who loved me and gave himself for me" (Galatians 2:20).

What a liberating truth this is! The pressure's off when we realize that the grace of God reveals our shortcomings not to condemn us but to take us to another level of freedom.

> # Escaping shame is not a once-and-done proposition.

Empowerment

Shame defines us if we let it. The decision is ours. Do we give power to the lies and shame or do we choose to rise above the noise and live by God's power instead? There is a purpose even in shame that God can use to redeem the messes we make. There is a better way.

The onerous power of shame that humiliates us can be turned into the very tool that liberates us. Humility arising from shame related to our own sinful behavior can lead us to repentance when we are empowered by God's love, grace, and truth. False humility from shame others place upon us or from self-imposed shame can be exposed. We can escape shame's clutches when we respond to conviction from the Holy Spirit and are free to admit our shortcomings and let go of labels that just don't stick anymore.

The stigma behind certain words can have shame attached to it. Single parent. Divorce. Sexual abuse. My heart still aches at those words, but not in the same manner it once did. The shame I felt from the misdeeds of another was not the story I had envisioned when I married a Christian and home educated my children, but sin or shame is not a respecter of persons. In an instant, our lives can change drastically when someone brings sin and shame into the picture. But that is not the end of the story. Our all-powerful God has overcome all of our shame. What we think is an end is

Shutting down shame without examination doesn't heal us.

just a beginning with our great God and Redeemer. What I thought was my destruction was His mighty deliverance. Romans offers a promise that we don't deserve, but what a promise it is: "And we know that in all things God works for the good of those who love him, who have been called according to his purpose" (8:28 NIV).

Yes, even when we feel forgotten and buried in shame, our God is not going to leave us in that place. Shame, the very thing we despise that seems to limit us all our days, can be used for our good when we humble ourselves and turn back toward God. But the choice is up to us. Condemnation is a powerful tool of the enemy, sometimes wrought at the hands of others and, surprisingly, sometimes by our own. But there is a Deliverer who wants to set us free from this tangled mess of shame. He invites us to examine ourselves and to heed the invitation that conviction brings, while letting go of condemnation's grip.

Shame Dismissed: Using the Biblical Lens

Encircled by men pressing in and yelling at her, ready to hurl stones upon her, the adulteress could only cower in a ball on the earth and wait for her punishment. Fully exposed, perhaps both physically and figuratively, she was completely broken and likely not expecting mercy that day. She did not anticipate that Jesus would first examine those who condemned her.

The response of God, who sees all, was radical:

They kept demanding an answer, so he stood up again and said, "All right, but let the one who has never sinned throw the first stone!" Then he stooped down again and wrote in the dust. When the accusers heard this, they slipped away one by one, beginning with the oldest, until only Jesus was left in the middle of the crowd with the woman. Then Jesus stood up again and said to the woman, "Where are your accusers? Didn't even one of them condemn you?" (John 8:7-10)

God came to take away not just our sin but our shame, too. The adulteress might have felt she deserved her punishment. She might have heaped shame upon herself. But God removed the condemnation from her accusers and her own heart. More than that, God removed His condemnation, too.

Like the adulteress, we can have shame for something we have done in our lives or that was done to us. People might also try to place more shame upon us. But when we invite the Master in and confess our sins before Him, our shame is removed, and our status renewed. We are no longer defined by shame and its many insidious devices. We are defined by our new identity, hidden in Christ (see Colossians 3:1-4). To have our identities "hidden in Christ" is to have them securely tucked away. Even if the world may drag us down and try to redefine who we are, our true identities cannot be changed. They are hidden (locked) in Christ.

I can hear some of you saying, "I wish it could be like that for me." It can, friend. But escaping shame is not a once-and-done proposition. As we explore the many different faces of shame in our lives, we will learn to remove the condemnation shame brings and accept God's gift to us as He takes the shame off you and me.

The Tools for Shame Removal

When we are willing to face our shame and use tools God gives us in His Word, shame no longer has dominion over us. Exposing shame reveals the root of blame. In examining the roots of our shame rather than pretending they do not exist, we can learn how to have shame off of us.

God's Word provides a safe place to examine shame and to learn why it has the effect it does on us. We form habits in relationships and respond without realizing that shame can be operating within our hearts and minds. Learning to see the patterns and presence of shame can help us eradicate it or respond to it in a biblical way, seeing it through a biblical lens.

Proverbs 11:2 tells us that "When pride comes, then comes disgrace, but with humility comes wisdom." The typical response to remove shame from us has been steeped in pride. We can be insulted that someone would try to shame us or be embittered by other people's judgment. Our response can be sinful as we try to project onto others the shame someone else or our own soul is directing to us. Shame upon shame. Shame will not disappear with pride.

What if we were to examine shame instead of being put off by it? Using a three-pronged biblical approach for dealing with shame, we can peel the tentacles of shame off our souls and examine the roots behind our shame through the lenses of truth, humility, and grace.

Review and Reflection

Truth

Through truth, we ask God to reveal if there is any truth in the accusation of shame knocking on the door of our minds.

Shame keeps us in bondage, but the truth sets us free. Yielding our perspective and submitting to truth, we step out of shame and into freedom. At first it is hard to even consider if any of the shame fits. We don't want to acknowledge its presence long enough to discover if there is any truth we need to receive. But shutting down shame without examination doesn't heal us. Maybe there is a component of the shame that we need to own. This does not mean we are defined by shame. Rather, it means when we acknowledge our weakness the shame dissolves as we apply God's truth to the presence of shame in our lives. God removes shame through truth when we are willing to be honest and teachable rather than defensive and prideful. Truth roots out shame: "Instead, speaking the truth in love, we will grow to become in every respect the mature body of him who is the head, that is, Christ" (Ephesians 4:15 NIV).

Humility

Through humility, we recognize that we are capable of shameful deeds. We understand that there is nothing good in us except Christ alone: "Therefore, as God's chosen people, holy and dearly loved, clothe yourselves with compassion, kindness, humility, gentleness and patience" (Colossians 3:12 NIV).

Even when we have determined that the shame does not fit us this time, we are humble enough to pause and consider if it does and thank God and give Him the glory when it doesn't. Keenly aware that we are capable of inviting shame into our lives, we thank God that He has removed it from us.

Grace

Through truth and humility, we ask for and receive the grace of God for what we need to learn from shame and gain the ability to filter out and let go of what we don't need. There is no condemnation for those who are in Christ Jesus, and we rejoice that God loves us enough to reveal both counterfeit and legitimate shame. And His grace is sufficient for us. "Three times I pleaded with the Lord to take it away from me. But he said to me, 'My grace is sufficient for you, for my power is made perfect in weakness.' Therefore I will boast all the more gladly about my weaknesses, so that Christ's power may rest on me" (2 Corinthians 12:8-9 NIV).

The beautiful thing about recognizing our shame and its ugly roots is also seeing the deliverance of our great God who does not leave us in shame but delivers us from its prison.

Examining the root of shame helps us deal with it biblically to:

- Uncover the shame we have concealed to begin to heal emotionally.
- Discover the hidden shame revealed to begin to deal with it biblically.
- Recover the original honor yielded to begin to feel real freedom.

Let's Recap

Shame is insidious. Whether it's fair or not, we can have shame for something we have done in our lives or that was done to us. The groups we trust most—church, family, coworkers, friends—can be sources of the most hurtful condemnation. Once we feel the sting of condemnation, shame moves into our mind. Shame is a head game, and we do it to ourselves. It affects our feelings of self-worth, our sense of empowerment, and makes us feel isolated. To be set free from shame we must learn to discern between conviction and condemnation and to replace the lie of shame with truth, humility, and grace that we can only get from God.

Reflection Questions

1. Have you ever felt like the adulteress woman? Surrounded by accusers? What did you feel in that moment?
2. Maybe there was a time when you were not even to blame. What was your response?
3. Why are accusations so powerful?

Name Your Shame—and Let It Go

DEVOTIONAL

Overcoming Shame's Condemnation

I prayed, "O my God, I am ashamed and embarrassed to
lift my face to you, my God! For our iniquities have climbed
higher than our heads, and our guilt extends to the heavens."
—*Ezra 9:6 (NET)*

Shame is invisible to the eye but palpable to the soul. It sneaks in through a perception we have of ourselves, brought on by other people's opinions (real or imagined), or our own opinion of ourselves based on our behaviors and belief system. Shame can be subtly woven into our daily existence, snuffing out joy, adding anxiety or fear. Shame can cause us to doubt God's goodness, fill our mind with futile thoughts, and wreck our health. It needs to be stopped.

Shame: We are not good enough as is. We are stuck in our shame with no way out. Maybe we are guilty of the shame we feel.

Shame Off You: We were made in the image of God. When we accepted His salvation, it changed us for all eternity. When we fix our hope on Christ, shame loses its power. And when we confess our shortcomings before a Holy God, He forgives us completely. Nothing else and no one else can ever condemn us. Ever.

What shame does is not as important as what God can do when we share our shame with Him. Shame off you, friend. Shame off me, too.

A Prayer

Lord, help me identify the shame in my life and to let it go. May I identify with you alone.

CHAPTER THREE

Shame's Roots

Exposing and Understanding the Real Cause of Shame

> *Then God said, "Let us make human beings in our image, to be like us. They will reign over the fish in the sea, the birds in the sky, the livestock, all the wild animals on the earth, and the small animals that scurry along the ground."... Now the man and his wife were both naked, but they felt no shame.*
> —Genesis 1:26, 2:25

> Worshiping at the throne of acceptance prevents us from pleasing God. —*Denise*

Walking into the room, I surveyed the landscape and looked down, wanting to avoid eye contact. Perhaps it was to avoid being known. If the eyes are a mirror to the soul, maybe someone would look into them and say that I was not enough. These people did not even know me. It was the DMV, for crying out loud. It wasn't a formal dance. But looking in the mirror before entering the building, I felt less than. My hair was dry and tousled, my makeup was not done. It was just me. In baggy sweatpants. Suddenly aware of my humble presence, I wondered what on earth had made me think it was OK to go out in public looking like this. *I don't know anyone here*, I thought. *It does not matter.* But it did.

This feeling of inferiority? Social anxiety formed in rejection and comparison, manifesting itself as shame. And what was I doing and thinking as I looked around me, as well? Hmmm. I guess I was also defining people's worth and shame quotient by their appearance or behavior. Ouch. How did it come to this? We live in a culture of shame. Our acceptance and confidence are fragile as the roots of shame are felt everywhere. The problem is, we don't often see it as shame, so we misdiagnose our condition and treat the wrong symptoms, hoping we can get rid of that nagging feeling dragging our soul down.

> The root of our shame is formed by a fear of rejection and cultivated by comparison.

The core root of our shame is formed by a fear of rejection and cultivated by comparison. As long as I can remember, rejection has played a role in my life. I desperately wanted to measure up to whatever the latest standard was, but never felt I could. And that standard just kept changing, just when I thought I had it figured out. The roots to this rejection were formed from a desire to be known and celebrated and feeling so very marginalized. I was a very shy little girl, the youngest of three with two older brothers I admired so much. They were not afraid to try anything. As they became star athletes, I struggled behind and tried to look athletic while I chased after the bats they threw. (Just call me Bat Girl, only I was not a superhero). I wanted to make my family proud, but I did not have the skills others had, so I chose to play the tuba. Nerd alert. Only problem was, the tuba was bigger than I was. The struggle was real as I tried to carry my instrument with all that my four-foot-eleven body could muster. The band director had mercy on me and suggested I try a smaller instrument: the euphonium. And so I did. And I played that thing every day. I had an occupation. A purpose. An identity. Granted, maybe many would not be trying to get the identity of a little girl puffing her cheeks playing a brass instrument, but I finally had something that I could do, and I could do it well.

At the root of shame is the belief that what we have is not enough.

While my world around me became crazy as my parents divorced, remarried other people, and divorced again, I blew a lot of hot air into that instrument. When birthdays came and went without a birthday call or card from my dad, I took those feelings of rejection and let them fuel my passion for music instead. It wasn't that my dad intended to hurt me. Divorce just shatters families. But my little girl heart took it as rejection. I was not enough. When I was mocked on the school bus and threatened again and again to be beaten up because of the color of my skin (I was the only *gringa* on the school bus), I stuffed the rejection that stifled my joy and poured my pain into the only thing I knew would give me the acceptance I longed for. Only problem was, the empty ache inside was not quelled by music. It was just pacified temporarily, substituting the shame I felt for being inferior, with the brief, temporary satisfaction of achievement. I was deceived into thinking that I could find what I was looking for in something other than my relationship with God. Even though it seemed good, nothing could satisfy my needs like only God could. The apple does not fall too far from the tree, it seems.

A Deceptive Promise

That apple in Eden must have been mighty good. OK, we are not sure whether it was an apple, but the forbidden fruit was so tempting that it seemed worthy of forsaking all the incredible blessings surrounding Adam and Eve. For what? For knowledge. I personally love learning, but knowledge of evil is something I would rather not know about. God feels the same way. He was not being a spoilsport to say that they could not have that piece of tantalizing fruit. He wanted them to live shame-free. Once they acquired knowledge of good and evil, they would become aware of their shortcomings, and suddenly judgmental comparison and all its shame would enter the world.

I think about Eve being able to be in the buff and not worry about whether her figure was perfectly toned. Pretty sure she did not have make up on, either. But she traded that perfection of shame-free living for an insecure world filled with shame. Of course, the proposition she was offered was not billed that way. It never is. It was couched in a positive light. She and Adam would be like God. But wait a minute, didn't God already say that He had made them in His image? What was this new, more improved version they craved?

This is how we get sucked into lives of shame, too. At the root of shame is the belief that what we have is not enough. Though we might not say such a thing, our hearts betray us. Discontentment with who we are or what we have comes from unfulfilled expectations. While we might not think of ourselves as being entitled, there can be a root of entitlement that thinks we deserve more. True contentment is not a natural emotion, after all. The apostle Paul even said he learned the secret of being content:

> I rejoiced greatly in the Lord that at last you renewed your concern for me. Indeed, you were concerned, but you had no opportunity to show it. I am not saying this because I am in need, for I have learned to be content whatever the circumstances. I know what it is to be in need, and I know what it is to have plenty. I have learned the secret of being content in any and every situation, whether well fed or hungry, whether living in plenty or in want. I can do all this through him who gives me strength. (Philippians 4:10-13 NIV)

Contentment cannot come from achieving our desire, but in asking Christ to meet us in our place of need, to strengthen us whether we are recipients of favor or rejection. Craving acceptance from man is never satisfied and only breeds shame. A whole room of people can be giving us favor, but the one person who rejects us is the one we remember. Someone did not think we were all that. We can let their opinion and definition of us burden our souls. Our victory over rejection depends on our belief and trust in God over man. At the root of our personhood is the lie that how we were made is somehow deficient. We need something else. Something better. This root of shame shows up in the funniest of places—in the pinnacle moments of life as well as in the trivial or mundane. And we see it in the lives of God's people played out over and over again.

Rejection's Roots

In this fallen world, we yearn for fairness and equality, yet want to be the favored one. Sometimes at the root of our quest for acceptance is a desire to be the most popular. We want admiration, maybe even praise. Pride fuels this desire and can turn the sting of rejection into a monster. Jacob wanted his brother Esau's birthright. He got it, all right. But we do reap what we sow, and the consequences of his envy were played out in his life, too. Though Jacob loved Rachel, he was tricked into marrying Leah and then ultimately had both as wives.

This was not an enviable position for the wives or for Jacob. Leah was not Jacob's favorite, and the sting of her not measuring up to Rachel's status visited her heart and mind every waking moment. It fueled her jealousy, pain, and depression and led to her participation in a battle with her sister for acceptance from Jacob. Leah tried to satiate her desperate pursuit of being the favorite with competition and achievement. She was going to have the most children. She was going to win Jacob's prized favor. But at what cost? The relationship with her sister and her peace of mind. Doubtful that she achieved her objective, Leah's obsession with besting her sister in childbearing ultimately cost her that sister. And the conflict in that household was intense. Sometimes in the pursuit of favor we lose sight of what really matters most. Sure, it stunk that Leah was given to a man who did not love her. But it was not Rachel's

> **Performing our way out of the feelings of shame is a flawed solution and another root of shame.**

fault. It stunk for Rachel, too. She did not want to have to share her husband.

The striving of man can steal our joy unless we accept the portion God has given to us. Instead of wanting someone else's portion, we can ask God to see His purposes that are far beyond our own self-oriented goals. God has placed us uniquely where we are supposed to be in this fallen world. Nothing is out of His control. The thorn in our flesh that plagues us? It is an opportunity to choose joy in the midst just like our Savior did when He carried His cross. When we do not gain favor, perhaps God is calling us elsewhere. Or maybe He is using that rejection to shape our character for another assignment. Worshiping at the throne of acceptance prevents us from pleasing God. Galatians reminds us that pleasing man is not our goal in this life, and seeking that favor above God's causes us to live our lives in vain: "For am I now seeking the approval of man, or of God? Or am I trying to please man? If I were still trying to please man, I would not be a servant of Christ" (1:10 ESV).

Rejection's Purpose

Rejection speaks over the framework of our little world and limits us according to that definition. We long for favor to relieve us from the heavy burden of someone else's limiting belief about our value or worth. Living with rejection is hard, indeed. If anyone can relate, it is Joseph. His own brothers despised him because of the favor God had given him. Yep. Jealousy. Who can stand before it? No one. Unless God is standing with you. Joseph's brothers really let their jealousy get the better of them, to the point of contemplating Joseph's death. Extreme rejection, for sure. Influenced by their envy, they sold Joseph into slavery and faked his death to hinder old dad from hoping that his favored son was still alive. In the desperate moments of rejection, God's purposes are always greater than any humiliation we may feel.

It isn't that God did not care about the unfair treatment; in fact, when we see the end of the story, we see that God used what Joseph's brothers meant for evil in powerful ways to save His people. But sometimes in the middle of rejection it is hard to see beyond our pain. We don't see any purpose in it whatsoever. When man rejects us, it might just be an assignment from God. Understanding the root of rejection can help to point us to where our acceptance should come from. When we respond to rejection with humility and perseverance, we are accepted in God's sight and God is glorified. We might even see God work in miraculous ways. Being still and trusting the Lord to fight our battles is so very hard when we are used to fighting our own battles or trying to perform to escape rejection's label. Our Savior chose the rejection we want to avoid. As we believe in Him and look to Him for acceptance, our shame is removed.

Rejection's Performance

We try to avoid rejection by being perfect. Performing our way out of the feelings of shame stemming from our very personhood is a flawed solution and another root of shame. Shame is a taskmaster. It commands us to try and fulfill its demands, yet the target is ever-changing. The performance that rendered us shame-free yesterday no longer fulfills the demands of being shame-free tomorrow. And this taskmaster is seemingly invisible, as we give shaming/rejecting power to anyone and everyone when we are a people pleaser at heart. While we work at our performance tiringly, Jesus is calling out to our hearts to rest. It's OK that we will never measure up. He accepts us anyway. Still, our flesh longs for those around us to give us the shame-free status. But they never can. The inferiority we feel is not from them after all.

Know Thyself: Rejection's Surprise

Blaming others for their shaming or shunning is never going to give us the confidence and clear conscience we crave. We discover in all our searching for acceptance from others that it really has never been other people's fault. But I can hear you say that it most certainly is. People can be so cruel and can communicate our lack of worth rather clearly and painfully. But we gave them that power. The insecurity from within, cultivated by comparison or a standard we feel we are supposed to ascribe to, is often at the root of our own shame. Peer pressure is not just for the school yard. It is prevalent throughout all of the stages of life as we seek to define ourselves by those around us. But when we know ourselves in light of Scripture, we can silence the voices of peers and ourselves from allowing rejection to limit us.

Taking inventory of our thoughts and behaviors, we can ask God for discernment to understand why we respond to acceptance and rejection the way we do. Rejection need not produce shame if we understand the heart behind the rejection and our response to it. Knowledge behind the motives of our response to shame is more powerful than the shame itself. But understanding alone cannot overcome shame. Applying understanding in our lives by the grace of God and through His Word gives us strength to overcome the shame stemming from rejection.

As we seek to know ourselves, we will more clearly see aspects that might seem shame-worthy. But we can choose to see ourselves through God's eyes instead of our own. We know our weaknesses not to self-deprecate, but to humble ourselves and to see Christ glorified in our weakness. In our weaknesses, we are strong when we let go of putting confidence in the flesh and put it in Christ instead. When we confess our weaknesses and give them to God, we make room for His power to be displayed in us and shame falls off of us. Once we have understood the root cause of our shame, we can choose the best route to get rid of these debilitating roots of shame in our lives.

> We can be more powerful than shame when we let go of the rejection from man and instead receive Christ's acceptance.

The Route and "Root" of Shame

The typical route of shame works like this: an event (comparison, judgment, rejection, for example) makes us *feel* shame, and we begin to *process* it. We may try to avoid feeling the shame by denying the shame, trying harder (performance) or deflecting the blame until we have layers of shame piled on top of one another. As we hide one shame, we are inviting another shame in. Building shame upon shame, our vision becomes clouded and we struggle to recognize legitimate shame from false shame. We begin to accept it all—the shame wrongly applied to us and the shame we earned all on our own—because we just don't want to have to deal with it.

Once we are aware of shame in our lives, we begin to process that shame by viewing it through one of two lenses: the condemning lens or the biblical lens.

Condemning Lens	**Biblical Lens**
Denial and rationalization	Confession and repentance
Hiding and guilt	Shame Off You!
Deeper shame and condemnation	Restoration

The condemning lens takes us down a path of denial and rationalization as we seek to hide the guilt plaguing our souls and continues to even more shame and condemnation if we continue on that path. But there is another route we can take that begins when we process our shame with truth, humility, and grace. When we examine the shame and confess or repent for our part in it, we remove shame rather than being condemned by it and are restored.

The route we take does not necessarily get to the root of shame. We take the typical, condemning route of shame innocently enough. We might have learned how to process it first by those around us. We learn quickly enough that shame is not something we want. But our coping and dismissal methods are faulty, inherited by fallen people. Rather than trying to understand how we got onto the route of shame in the first place by examining the root of the problem, we would rather quickly and quietly silence its outward expression. But underneath, the root of our shame is bubbling and will eventually surface. Shame might be manifest as sorrow on the outside but on the inside there could be a host of roots contributing to that sorrow: jealousy, unforgiveness, anger, hurt feelings, abuse, lack of self-worth, doubting God. The list goes on and on. When we try to silence the shame without examining these roots, we continue on the cycle of shame unless somewhere we recognize the real root behind our shame and the dysfunctional patterns we developed to cope with it. A lot of these mechanisms we put into place without realizing it, often arising from childhood, where we responded to shame around us, sometimes in unhealthy ways.

A Healed Daughter

One of the most significant roots of shame in my life came from rejection. I did not realize the profound effect that rejection from father figures played in my life until recently. My father's absence as a by-product of divorce hurt deeply while I was growing up, but it was compounded by the outright rejection from other father figures who persecuted me for my faith and the decision to home educate my children. That rejection ripped me apart.

I understand now that it was a spiritual battle. These father figures did not understand what being born again meant, though years later, one of these men apologized for his behavior and admitted that I was the most authentic believer he had ever encountered. It is a wonderful thing when God brings situations around, but that is not always the case. In the middle of our pain from the rejection of man, God wants to meet our need. He wants to be our Abba Father when our earthly fathers wound us. I desperately wanted a father's affection and found it on my knees, crying and praying to my heavenly Father. Having my needs met in Him first enabled me to accept my earthly fathers as they were.

Lack of acceptance from family is particularly painful. They supposedly know us best. But rejection is spiritual, a battle of the soul. It does not really have to do with us at all. People reject others when their flesh dominates their minds. Or sometimes we misunderstand and think we are being rejected when we are not. When we wait on God and trust Him for deliverance, He is always faithful. His timing just might not be ours. We aren't sure when David penned Psalm 27, but the character shaped during the rejection David felt left a lasting impression on him, as well as the ensuing consequences from David's own sin and shame. David waited on His God. And God delivered.

> Though my father and mother forsake me, the LORD will receive me. Teach me your way, LORD; lead me in a straight path because of my oppressors. Do not turn me over to the desire of my foes, for false witnesses rise up against me, spouting malicious accusations. I remain confident of this: I will see the goodness of the LORD in the land of the living. Wait for the LORD; be strong and take heart and wait for the LORD. (Psalm 27:10-14 NIV).

Rather than striking back with vengeance or permitting bitterness to rob us of the abundant life Christ promises, we can be more powerful than shame when we choose to let go of the rejection from man and receive Christ's acceptance instead.

Who's Got the Power?

Shame is powerful. At the root, we see that shame is potent because it is wielded among so many. But the power one exudes by shaming others reveals one's own weaknesses instead. Insecure people shame others. When we are shamed by an insecure person, we need to recognize that they bear the shame that they are trying to cast upon us. Seeing the truth behind shame helps us to overcome it and use it in a redemptive way. Rather than letting shame turn into resentment, hurt, or bitter feelings, we can powerfully choose to forgive those who shamed us and pray for them. Their shaming does not apply to us unless we let it. When we feel rejected and hated, we are in good company. Our Savior showed us the way. Hated without cause, he patiently relied on God and waited for the Spirit of truth to defend Him: "If the world hates you, know that it has hated me before it hated you. If you were of the world, the world would love you as its own; but because you are not of the world, but I chose you out of the world, therefore the world hates you" (John 15:18-20 ESV).

Review and Reflection

Truth

Finding the cause of our shame does not produce shame, but helps us to extinguish it.

Humility

When we understand the roots of our shame and are willing to expose them, we are not shamed, but healed.

Grace

No matter what the root cause is of our shame, all shame can be healed through our great Savior, the Holy Spirit, prayer, and the Word of God.

Let's Recap

Understanding the real cause of shame sets us free. Shame is essentially an endless cycle of discontentment and comparison, in which we reject ourselves or are rejected by others when our comparison falls short of the ideal. Examples of this sort of comparison include judgmentalism, fear of rejection, seeking acceptance from others, peer pressure, jealousy, anger, unforgiveness, and insecurity. To avoid feeling the shame, we rationalize, become people pleasers, blame others, or practice avoidance and hiding. However, these are not useful mechanisms. Instead, we should ask God for discernment/understanding, learn our weaknesses, trust God's purposes, and see ourselves, then, through God's eyes.

Reflection Questions

1. What root of shame do you identify with the most? Can you trace its beginning?
2. How will you silence the root of shame in your life?
3. What new roots can you form in your life to counter the habitual roots of shame in your life?

Name Your Shame—and Let It Go

DEVOTION

Shame Off Rejection

And after you have suffered a little while, the God of all grace, who has called you to his eternal glory in Christ, will himself restore, confirm, strengthen, and establish you.
—1 Peter 5:10 (ESV)

Rejection is one of the most significant roots of shame. But it need not define us if we see it for what it is. This isn't easy; it's far easier to believe the lies rejection tells us: that there is something wrong with us or that we are forever defined by it.

The list of shame by rejection can go on and on. Rejection is a part of life. Acceptance is a part of faith. So let go of others' definition of you and pick up God's instead. Believing that our heavenly Father is good, loving, and accepting sets us free to accept ourselves, too.

Shame stemming from rejection is an indicator that we are trying too hard to perform to earn acceptance that God already gave us. When we just keep standing and let God defend us, our rejection melts away in light of His grace. Just keep doing the next, best, right thing and let the Lord take care of our shame. It doesn't matter what rejection we have experienced in the past. Today is a new day. Walk in the freedom of Christ—shame off us, friends.

A Prayer

Lord, help me fully embrace the acceptance you offer and let go of the rejection this world gives. Set me free from shame and all of its roots, that I may live the abundant life You promise in Your Word.

CHAPTER FOUR

Shame's Cycles

How to Choose a Shame-Free Life

At that moment their eyes were opened, and they suddenly felt shame at their nakedness. So they sewed fig leaves together to cover themselves. —Genesis 3:7

We will never be set free from shame unless we are willing to face it head on. —*Denise*

I was around six years old when I first remember feeling shame so deep I wanted to disappear. Family members had brought me to a nude beach and I was the only one clothed. "Go ahead, you can take off your clothes, it's OK here." No way. No siree. Not this girl. "Just take your top off then." My brothers hit the waves and told me I better not look out at them. No need to worry about that—I had no desire to look at them. Something was not right. Why were all of these people naked? Looking down at the sandy shore and shielding my eyes from the environment surrounding me, I longed for the moment when we could finally leave.

I had not done anything wrong, but the stigma of guilt stayed with me. Shame is a consequence of living in a fallen world. But sometimes shame is projected upon us through no fault of our own. This misplaced shame can hang on us like a wet rag, but it is not as disingenuous as the shame people cast on each other every day through false guilt and manipulation. Shame is an assault on the very core of who we are. It assassinates our character, tries to define us, and says there is no hope. Scrambling to cover our shame, we reach for our own fig leaves and try to hide our shame like Adam and Eve did. But hiding shame never heals it. Like an infectious disease, hidden or long-buried, shame inhibits growth and can even destroy lives, but we can learn how to overcome it.

> Shame is a powerful tool of the enemy used to keep people on a cycle of shame.

Lifelong Shame Becomes Habit

It is not just the root of shame that we have to recognize, but the perpetuation of shame in our lives. We are creatures of habit and sometimes those habits can be our undoing. Like hamsters on a wheel, we can get so busy that we don't look up to see where we are going. Changing our behavior is not an easy feat, especially as it pertains to shame. Lifelong shame becomes a habit, and we cycle through the stages of shame over and over again.

Without realizing it, we can be enveloped and crippled by a culture of shame. We adapt to it because it is all we know. Shame imprisons its victims without their realizing the effect and toll that it is exacting. The power of shame's hold is deepened by the cycle of shame, which seems impossible to escape. That day on the nude beach was just one moment, but it affected me in profound ways. It rattled the security I thought I had, that suddenly everyone could be exposed. I felt shame that day, rather than the freedom many of those people seemed to be feeling. And I carried that shame forward. I had to find a way to cover myself, to cover my shame in this life whenever I faced it. I never wanted to be so exposed again; I did not want anyone to see my flaws or to see what I did not want to show. The cycle of shame had begun in my life, only I did not know it.

> God did not come to condemn us, but to reveal His salvation.

The cycle of shame begins as a focus on self, in particular, our lack of worth in some specific area of our lives or a general feeling of inadequacy. Because shame is not always recognized as shame at its inception, we might not also be aware that it has become a part of how we live. Some aspects of the cycle of shame are learned and others are reinforced in a culture that seems designed to keep people trapped in shame. Some shame is inherited or learned. Some shame is misplaced, but all shame can be traced through its cyclic pattern. What makes the cycle of shame so powerful in its hold on us? Back to us being creatures of habit. We grow accustomed to our patterns of shame and find it difficult to be set free from them.

Our response to shame can change the course of our life. Shame is a powerful tool of the enemy used to subjugate people and keep them in a state of oppression, continuously on a cycle of shame. The enemy seeks to bind us in sin and uses shame to keep us from seeing our need for forgiveness. God can use the shame that results from sin to bring His people back to Himself. While the enemy condemns us by using shame as one of his main weapons, the Holy Spirit convicts our souls and invites us to discard shame altogether. Having the discernment to know the difference between condemnation and conviction gives us the ability to recognize and reject shame in its many hidden forms and embrace the voice of God instead. Accepting conviction from the Holy Spirit sets us free from a cycle of shame. Being reminded of the goodness of God and His purposes also releases us from the cycle of condemnation. God did not come to condemn us, but to reveal His salvation and remove our condemnation. "For God did not send his Son into the world to condemn the world, but in order that the world might be saved through him" (John 3:17 ESV). Shame does not happen in a vacuum. When shame is welling up within our own hearts or is wrought by the hands of others, we have a choice of which route we will take: the cycle of the condemned or the way of freedom and restoration.

Maybe you have not experienced the severity depicted at the end of the cycle of shame, but you are beginning to recognize that you have shame in your life in one way or another. Shame off you, friend. There is no shame in admitting that we have shame. Professing that we don't have shame when this universal stigma is so prevalent will likely accelerate our trip down the route of shame circling round and round on the cycle of shame. And now, to be set free in Jesus's name.

The Cycle of Shame

The Cycle of Shame—that hamster wheel of habit—repeats as we become more and more overcome by the burden of guilt. The root of our shame begins to grow ugly fruit, while the four Cs of the Cycle of Shame keep us circling about the shame in our lives as we attempt to resolve shame on our own.

- Condemnation
- Comparison
- Crisis
- Commitment

Condemnation

↗

Commitment   Cycle of Shame   Comparison

↖   ↘

Crisis

Condemnation

Condemnation causes us to try a multitude of methods in an attempt to cover our shame. No one wants to be labeled as being shameful. Well, I guess there are those in our society who have been on the cycle so long, they plunge headlong into a prideful "shameless" way of life. Rather than trying to diagnose and resolve the shame in their lives, they give in to it or disregard the Spirit of conviction.

Most of us, though, are left dealing with the fruits of the condemnation phase of the cycle: accusation, guilt, and shame heaped on shame. We want to hide rather than deal with it, but no amount of trying to convince ourselves that being in shame is preferable to being set free will ever bring healing. No, we have to face the condemnation and be willing to examine it.

Comparison

When condemnation is knocking on the door of our souls, the first reaction is to compare ourselves with other people's level of shame or to deny it altogether. Somehow, feeling like we are in the company of others feeling shame makes us feel better about our own shame. Their shame is worse, right? This comparison phase bears fruit too: we rationalize, we project, we blame others. We engage in denial. But no amount of comparison can free our souls. Our shame is our own, compounded by the shame others are trying to place on us. We stand alone before God.

Crisis

There is a moment on the cycle of shame during which we reach a crisis. Our methods aren't working. Our shame is still facing us in the mirror we look into each day or plaguing our thoughts. It is at this stage that we decide how we are going to cope with the reality of the damaging effects of shame.

The fruits of the crisis phase can go either way: we might continue with denial into disbelief or we might go into hiding, pretending it doesn't exist. However, the crisis might provide revelation: we might embrace the truth of our shame. This type of revelation could provide a way out for those who finally begin to see that their methods are futile, but it typically leads to discouragement and a worsened state of shame.

Commitment

We might try to get up and move forward, insisting that our shame is in the past, but when shame is not dealt with and eradicated, it can affect our resolve to rise above shame. Certainly we want to put shame behind us, but ironically, our commitment to be shame-free is impeded by the very behaviors—habits—we have developed to deal with the shame in our lives.

Thus, the fruits of the commitment phase—when we're hurt, when we're angry, when we're bitter—put us right back on the hamster-wheel cycle of shame. We are handicapped to truly move past shame because it has metastasized into every area of our lives. Like a cancer we thought was isolated to one part of our lives, shame begins to affect and color our whole being. Unless we commit to a biblical solution, our commitment to rise above shame without positive and concrete ways of dealing with it becomes a commitment to stay on the cycle instead.

The root of our shame is beneath the surface, bearing ugly condemning fruit in each stage of The Cycle of Shame. People try to get rid of shame in the wrong way: with pride, rationalization, or dismissal without dealing with it. But these methods do not get rid of the underlying issues. Shame keeps haunting its victims until it is dealt with biblically. All shame, merited and unmerited, should be evaluated through a biblical lens. Doing so places us on another cycle—the cycle of restoration.

Condemnation
- Accusation
- Guilt
- Shame

Comparison
- Rationalization
- Contemplation
- Denial
- Projection/Blame

Crisis
- Revelation
- Unbelief/Belief
- Hiding
- Embracing

Commitment
- Bitterness
- Anger
- Hurt
- Shame

The Cycle of Shame Off You

Cycles aren't all bad when they are formed using the biblical lens of truth, humility, and grace. The four Rs of the Shame-Off-You cycle lead us continually to the presence of God for shame removal.

- Revelation
- Reflection
- Repentance
- Restoration

Revelation

No one likes to be exposed. We would rather hide than have to face the reality of yet another flaw. But revelation is a gift to those willing to receive it. Rather than viewing revelation as a pathway to condemnation, we see it as necessary exposure to bring conviction and healing. Sometimes it is the method of the revelation itself that we don't appreciate. Perhaps someone did not approach us in love. Or maybe the shame is displaced and not warranted at all. Our self-esteem has been chipped at for so long we feel that we cannot bear to be vulnerable enough to examine the newest shame presenting itself at the door of our heart and mind. However, we will never be set free from shame unless we are willing to face it head on.

When our shame is revealed, we can feel as if we are the only one steeped in shame; the only one facing the temptation to remain in our shame. But we are reminded that we are all the same. We all will face temptations, but God always makes a way out: "No temptation has overtaken you that is not common to man. God is faithful, and he will not let you be tempted beyond your ability, but with the temptation he will also provide the way of escape, that you may be able to endure it" (1 Corinthians 10:13 ESV).

Temptation does not always have to yield to sin. Temptation might also be unrecognized. Negative behaviors, self-deprecation, condemnation, fear, and anxiety all plague the heart of mankind. Thank God that He has made a way out!

Reflection

Meditating on shame is a two-way street. We can choose to contemplate on the condemnation and our guilt, obsessing over the shame others or ourselves are ascribing to us. Or we can meditate on shame through an entirely different lens. Focusing on what God can accomplish with our shame, rather than on man or the enemy, redeems shame and uses it to shape our character instead of condemning it. We see the fruit from being willing to search our hearts, especially when it leads us to repentance:

> As it is, I rejoice, not because you were grieved, but because you were grieved into repenting. For you felt a godly grief, so that you suffered no loss through us. For godly grief produces a repentance that leads to salvation without regret, whereas worldly grief produces death. For see what earnestness this godly grief has produced in you, but also what eagerness to clear yourselves, what indignation, what fear, what longing, what zeal, what punishment! At every point you have proved yourselves innocent in the matter. (2 Corinthians 7:9-11 ESV)

Repentance

Shame is harmful unless we are able to deal with it biblically. The most common term for repentance in the New Testament is from Greek, *metanoia*, translated as repent, meaning to turn or return, to change your heart and mind. Turning would not be complete if we did not make a complete turn. When we repent and turn away from shame, we are free to replace the shame in our lives with its opposite: honor. Where there is a void as we turn from shame, the enemy will quickly try to replace it. But when we replace shame with an honorable deed, behavior, or belief, we silence shame's accusation. First John 1:9 holds a promise for those willing to confess their sins. God is faithful. No shame is too big for Him to deliver us from any and all sin and shame: "If we confess our sins, he is faithful and just to forgive us our sins and to cleanse us from all unrighteousness" (ESV).

Restoration

God has not just forgiven our sin and shame, but the guilt of it, too. The enemy is a deceiver and an accuser of the brethren. Overcoming the accusations of the enemy seems insurmountable, but not when we are rightly armed with God's Word and His precious promises. David knew what it was to be in shame. He committed adultery and murder. And lied about it. But David was still considered a man after God's own heart. He responded to the rebuke from God when he was guilty. And when he was not guilty but was relentlessly pursued by his enemies, he was humble and received it all from God's hand. This beautiful prayer uttered from the lips of David is such a reminder that God does not just forgive our iniquity, but our guilt, also. This includes false guilt, too. "Then I acknowledged my sin to you and did not cover up my iniquity. I said, 'I will confess my transgressions to the LORD.' And you forgave the guilt of my sin" (Psalm 32:5 NIV).

> It is only when we recognize shame that we can do something about it.

Innocence Gone

As a little girl standing on that beach with the sun beaming down on me, more than just shame was exposed that day. A part of my innocence was taken that could not be replaced. Shame steals our innocence and makes us feel there is no way out. Confined by shame's definition, we struggle to get out but don't know the way.

I can imagine the emotion Adam and Eve must have felt when they were standing in the garden of Eden suddenly realizing their nakedness. Once sin entered the world, shame did, too.

They suddenly became aware of their condition and tried to cover their shame with leaves. I wanted to *leave* the shameful surroundings I was thrust into on the beach that day. But trying to escape or cover our shame only allows it to grow. Unless we are willing to lift the rug and expose our shame, we will never recover from the damaging effects of shame.

The saddest moment of history, when man fell, probably looked like one of the funniest. Attired in plants, they tried to play it off like it was just another day in the Garden. Adam might even have been whistling, pretending everything was fine. The only problem is, the One who had created them knew that they had not needed to wear clothing before. While Adam and Eve were hiding, shame was growing. I wonder if they really thought they would get away with tricking God as they cowered in the bushes.

But God had a plan to remove their shame. While we attempt to hide our shame, God always provides a remedy. In a fallen world where shame is embedded in our culture, God is working to restore us back to the state before we felt shame. The God who removed the curse of sin can also remove the consequence of shame from our souls and in our daily lives. While we tend to look at our circumstances in the present, God knows the end.

There were consequences that day in the garden that we still feel today, but the goodness of our God also met shame personified in the Garden that day and made a promise that shame would one day be defeated. A plan was put in place that would secure the dignity of man again and remove any residual shame. Still, sometimes we can feel like shame's grasp cannot be overcome. Consequences can be painful and at times we believe that our freedom from shame is not fully possible.

There is a biblical approach to living shame-free, but as always, there are obstacles that might distract us from God's ability to remove all of our shame.

Obstacle 1: Pride

Pride keeps us from admitting that we might have shame to own up to. It also prevents us from ridding ourselves of false shame. Somehow, we forget that it is only God's grace in us that makes us righteous and we can revert back to the tendency of trying to earn our righteous standing. But denying shame will not make us righteous. Confessing our shame with humility enables us to grasp what we need to and let go of what we don't.

Obstacle 2: Failure to Recognize

As we have seen from the cycles and the levels of shame, it is only when we recognize shame that we can do something about it. Sometimes recognizing shame in our lives is not so easy. Shame is hidden within the framework of our culture and within our minds. But when we illumine our minds with the Word of God, the Holy Spirit convicts us and reveals what is hidden from our eyes.

Obstacle 3: Pain

We might be at such a wounded place that just functioning feels impossible. Worn down by our emotional pain, we can't see clearly enough to even know which way is up. I've been there. Just existing feels like being in a fog and trying to accomplish normal tasks feels like walking in mud. The enemy has beaten us down so severely, it is hard to get motivated.

But pain can become our deliverer if we know where to go. We were never meant to muster our own will power apart from God's will. When we seek Him through the pain, our great God transforms it into a pathway of deliverance. We likely did not recognize our need for deliverance until pain came sharply knocking on our door. It hurts, but the comfort and healing God provides far outweighs temporary suffering that frees us from the shackles of shame.

Obstacle 4: Need for Acceptance

The innate desire within us to be accepted by others can also prevent us from applying a biblical approach to shame removal. When our focus is set on pleasing man, we polish the outside and hide any potential shame. But when our heart is set to please God, we understand that He sees us completely and still accepts us. It is OK to acknowledge our shame. We don't need to hide it anymore. This revelation—that exposing shame can set us free to be who we were created to be—gives us the acceptance we longed for. God restores what shame stole. I did not realize just how much shame was controlling me before I went through intense suffering and sought recovery. From subtle negative comments from others to my own fear of people's perceptions; from medical issues to trying to perform my way out of shame; from disappointment to personal failure, my need for acceptance was an obstacle to a shame-free life.

Apply the Biblical Lens

Like a physician must diagnose the root of our illness to treat it, we must diagnose the root of our shame (see chapter 3) and overcome our own obstacles as we apply a biblical approach to break free from the cycle of shame. The solutions the world offers are temporary and often miss the target, but God's remedy is eternal and brings healing to our inner being. Our genius Creator knows what His creation needs most. We need to use biblical solutions that offer hope and healing rather than just saying we should not be ashamed. Finally, having a biblical worldview on shame limits the extent of shame and places a remedy within reach.

Review and Reflection

Truth

We will never be more accepted than we are now. God accepted us because of His mercy and not our performance.

Humility

We will not arrive at perfection down here, but in humility, we see that in our weaknesses, we are strong. Christ is our strength. And He will complete the work He has begun in us.

Grace

When we are accepted by God, we are free to accept others even when they do not accept us. When we look to our Savior rather than to our shame, we let go of the temporary and embrace the eternal. Our identity is in Christ now, not in our shame. Our shame does not define us when our Savior redeems us.

Let's Recap

Lifelong feelings of shame become habit, and unless we know how to stop it in its tracks, it becomes an endless cycle of condemnation, comparison, crisis, and commitment. Ultimately, it's all we know. At that point, the only way to break the cycle is to seek God—through revelation, reflection, repentance, and restoration. As in any undertaking, though, there will be obstacles (pride, failure to recognize, pain, and need for acceptance). Pride keeps us from admitting that we might have shame to own up to, while recognizing shame in our lives is not so easy. Pain wears us down and make it hard to gather the strength to resist shame, while our need for acceptance from man obscures our need for God.

Reflection Questions

1. What does it mean to you to be exposed? What is your typical response when you recognize you have been exposed in some way?
2. Maybe there was a time when you were not even to blame. What was your response?
3. Why are we afraid of exposure of our weaknesses?

Name Your Shame—and Let It Go

DEVOTIONAL

Shame Off Our Worldview

He said, "I heard the sound of you in the garden, and I was afraid because I was naked; and I hid myself." —Genesis 3:10 (ESV)

You don't have to hide anymore. Really, you don't. I don't either. We don't have to live in fear of shame, as if it defines us. Like Adam and Eve, we will recognize our need for a covering, but when we try to cover ourselves, it does not work out so well. Hiding shame does not heal it. And being aware of shame in our lives is the first step to healing.

Shame is a powerful tool of the enemy, used to distract and condemn us and keep us from being who we are created to be. Christ removed all of our shame and has set us free, but sometimes there are areas of our life that are clothed in shame and we may not even see it.

The world's view produces shame and leads to death. A biblical worldview produces hope and honor, stemming from the fear of God, and leads to life. The choice is up to us: Will we choose life or death? Will we opt for a life full of shame or the Shame-Off-You life?

A Prayer

God, it gets so confusing down here. Please bring clarity and reveal the hidden shame that blocks my view of the truth. Enable me to understand and to walk in your truth with humility and grace.

CHAPTER FIVE

Shame's Reach

How to Stop Shame's Impact

For the Scripture says, "Everyone who believes in him will not be put to shame." —Romans 10:11 (ESV)

Shame can't reach a forgiven soul. —*Denise*

Early in the morning while the sun's light was still hidden, my son walked into the room and found me crying out to God. Rising early was not an abnormal occurrence. I rise early to seek God before others are awake. But my son has a way of knowing when I am discouraged or burdened. "What's wrong, Mom?" he asked cheerfully. I began to tell him about accusations that someone in our community was spreading against me, to which he quickly retorted, "Shame Off You, Mom!"

This has become a common phrase in our home, as can be imagined. We are living out the principle of recognizing when false shame is being hurled our way and learning how to distinguish and extinguish it before it reaches our souls. Those three words have stopped the reach of shame in profound ways but it isn't so much the words as it is the mindset and new behavior we have learned in approaching shame.

Unfortunately, accusations and shaming are not rare occurrences in our culture. The behavior we hoped people would outgrow is not just confined to immature children on the school yard. It just isn't. Adults are just as much to blame as they look to advance in this world by controlling others through shame—putting them down or blaming them for their own problems. Add to this reality of shaming embedded in our culture the dynamic of internet and social media and we can have a shame-charged existence. The need to be able to process shame biblically is crucial in a social media–rich society.

Shame Has a Wide Reach Online

Numbly clicking through the posts on Facebook, we can become deadened to the reality of pain on the other side of the computer screens. People can hide behind their posts and comments; they often feel free to type things they might never have said to a person's face. It's sad. And the thing about words on a screen—they can be read by potentially scores of people, including the victim, multiple times. Shame reverberates in an environment like that. The old saying, "Sticks and stones may break my bones, but words will never hurt me," keeps coming around generation after generation, but we know now that words do wound, do break hearts, and do shame our existence. Yet the comments just keep coming. People chime in to hurl their proverbial stones, not cognizant or not caring what it might be doing to the other person.

Shaming is a form of bullying, which is often primarily about words. Growing up, I encountered bullies countless times. As much as I sought to avoid them, they still found me. Bullying in person is bad enough, but cyberbullying reaches us where we live—through social media. It's particularly prevalent among the young. You've seen the stories: young girls or boys—persecuted by other young girls and boys—who sometimes even commit suicide rather than face up to the torture they endure at school and online.

Death. All because people felt the need to put down others. The sad hollow feeling of being shamed and unloved haunts victims of shame and leaves them with an overwhelming sense of worthlessness. They listen to shame's lies that there is no way

> We give shame the power to harm us only when we let other people define our worth.

to overcome its stigma and allow the voices in their head to convince their souls that they need to end the pain. In extreme situations, some end the precious life God gave them, convinced that there is no escape from shame's reach. Even if we cognitively understand how to process shame, it can still reach us in debilitating ways.

What a shame indeed. But the stigma and pain of shame doesn't have to stick. Children and adults can be equipped to counter shame and overcome it. Through the Word of God we can help determine the reach of shame in our lives. Additional steps can also be taken to help us remove the stigma of shame. Blocking out toxic people takes bravery, but it might be necessary for us to get clarity when we are overwhelmed by their negativity. Surrounding ourselves with godly believers also helps us to rise above the shamers.

We stop shame's reach by understanding how it operates. While shame has a profound effect on the human soul, and the reach of shame is prolific today (with the internet pumping and exposing salacious stories to the craving public), ultimately shame is powerful because we care too much what man thinks about us. We give shame the power to harm us only when we let other people define our worth.

> The human soul longs to be known and appreciated but shaming is being known and defamed.

Shame has the possibility of defining us or freeing us. The rollercoaster ride of acceptance and shame is a painful one when we receive incoming shame as truth. But if we adopt a biblical mind-set and review shame objectively, we have power over it. Developing a means of processing shame (see chapter 4 for the cycle of Shame Off You and chapter 2 for the biblical lens), we overcome shame rather than being overcome by shame. This requires subjecting our emotions to our will and not permitting shame to rule our hearts.

The shamed feel powerless when encountering accusations. Like a room full of people in which the loudest opinions tend to persuade others, shame can feel like a tidal wave engulfing us. What is it about this reach of shame that is so paralyzing? Why does it have such a damaging, profound effect? We crave acceptance as if it will prove our worth. And when we make a mistake and accusations ring true, we feel boxed in by others' definition of us because we know there is truth in their accusation and we doubt ourselves. We fail to recognize that just because there might be a hint of truth to the shame *does not mean we are condemned*. Still, it can seem as if there is no way out. Public shaming magnifies the accusation of shame we feel so deeply within our own soul. Numbers paralyze us, too.

So while the internet has the capability of spreading shame far and wide, the reach of shame is extended by our personal response to it. It might begin with the realization that we just don't fit in. We aren't popular. We feel inferior and others might be bullying or shunning us into that place. But shame reaches much further than the opinion of others. It arrests our thoughts, fills us with anxiety, and makes us feel trapped. Left alone, shame runs its course through a progression of levels…unless we stop it cold. Shame's reach is magnified as it morphs into a progression from embarrassment to social anxiety, depression, or worse.

The Shame Spectrum: Levels of Shame

We can't get rid of something we don't see or try to deny. Recognizing the shame in our lives and what level it is at can help us see the manifestation that shame is already exhibiting in our lives. Maybe you recognize yourself in the shame spectrum below.

Levels of Shame—Are You on This Spectrum?
1. Avoidance ("I need to hide it")
   Avoiding others or assuming a mask; pretense or
   misdirection

2. Self-righteousness ("I can cover it")
   Doing good works; comparing yourself to others
   Seeking counterfeit affection (praise, possessions,
        status)
3. Pride ("I must cover it")
   Judging others (assigning motives or attaching fault)
   Setting standards (clothes, car, career)
4. Rebellion ("I can't live in it")
   Escape or fantasy
   Risky behavior (danger, adrenaline, euphoria)[1]

It is easy to overlook shame in the early stages, but as we continue on the shame cycle, we begin to deepen our relationship with it and go further on the spectrum. From the simple shame of embarrassment we all experience to stifling shame that seems to impact every aspect of our lives, shame bears progressively uglier fruit that cripples us unless it is stopped. It is important to recognize not only that we are all on the shame spectrum but also where we are on it, because shame will continue to grow when it is unrecognized. The coping mechanisms we concoct to help us deal with shame become a dysfunctional crutch that entraps us on the spectrum.

Avoidance

Avoidance is the classic response to shame initially. This is the "flight" personality. Rather than fight the shame, the sufferer would

---

1. Tom Crandall, "Jesus Despised the Shame," A Broken & Contrite Heart (blog), May 18, 2015, www.contriteheart.org/shame-undone/jesus-despised -the-shame/#more-240.

rather avoid it because it is painful. But not dealing with shame at this level will only lead to a greater problem. Avoiding people or situations does not help us to heal. Neither does trying to overcome shame by trying to be perfect.

Self-Righteousness

We can begin to harden ourselves to shame's reality when we shut down the shame we are feeling and replace it with a sense of self-righteousness. This response is not so easy to detect. It just feels right. We feel justified. Rather than acknowledging the shame in the room, we begin to make excuses for it and to justify ourselves. We might even do amazing good works to try and make up for the shame that is plaguing us, not realizing that shame is controlling us through it all.

Pride

When shame is becoming more entrenched within our souls, we begin to respond to it with pride. We become desperate to eradicate shame and our association with it. Gloating about our shame or the opposite—minimizing it and boasting about something in us that is "less shameful"—cannot rid us of shame. Trying to achieve great things to shadow the less than glowing areas in our lives only leaves us empty. Faking it will never truly cover shame and pride only produces more shame. Proverbs reminds us: "When pride comes, then comes disgrace, but with humility comes wisdom" (11:2 NIV).

Rebellion

Humility can help us turn the corner, but pride is likely blocking our view and we don't see our need. Rebellion is at the end of the spectrum where we become exasperated with the presence of shame in our lives and try to convince ourselves that we don't care and that we actually enjoy our state of shame—deception at its worst. We begin to see counterfeit options as a means of an escape and lose perspective on reality—shame gone amok.

So where are you on the spectrum? Shame might be as simple as living in a culture of shame where we are manipulated or coerced into performing for others. Or maybe it is social shame. We are embarrassed that we don't measure up to the standards society sets. Shame could also emanate from a painful traumatic event in your life that has left you lost or diminished your self-worth. The avoidance of pain or other specific things that may trigger or amplify our sense of shame becomes our survival tactic. We may avoid a place or a person because it simply hurts too much. Later, our shame might evolve into fear and anxiety as we try to disregard or resolve the shame within us by covering it, but don't readily see its effect is steadily worsening. We might try to deny it altogether, spin it or rationalize it, or maybe displace it into being someone else's shame. Or shame could start to overtake us. We become absorbed in our painful

> It is not the truth about our guilt that matters, but the truth about what God did to our guilt. He bore it all.

reality, desperate to eradicate shame but plunge headlong into an even deeper state of shame. Anger and an offended spirit can then cause us to act in unhealthy ways to try and kill the shame we are bearing, but it is slowly killing us instead. At any place on the shame spectrum, we can get off the cycle of shame keeping us there. Shame loses its power when we find our identity in Christ instead of in our shame.

Your Dirty Laundry

We've all heard the phrase "Don't air your dirty laundry." In one sense, this principle is scriptural, meaning that grace covers our flaws rather than exposes them. Once they've been covered, there is no need to air them. In another sense, it can become a culture where sin and secrets breed shame—the "avoidance" level of shame. But bringing personal matters into the public eye is akin to making the public the judge and jury in our lives. We feel the seemingly omnipresent feeling of being known—in a bad light—with no way to defend ourselves. Who knows who all is aware of our story? And do they know the truth? The human soul longs to be known and appreciated, maybe even celebrated, but shaming is being known and defamed. I know, because it happened to me.

Standing in the family courtroom, facing the judge with my former in-laws right behind me, the stares and judgment from those accusing me made me feel like the adulterous woman must have felt surrounded by her accusers. Their piercing gaze burned a hole in my back. My clouded brain was burdened with excessive information, and I was filled with anxiety as I walked up to the witness stand. I tried to grasp the intent behind their line of questioning. Constantly needing to be prepared with an answer to the deeply probing questions, I wished I could disappear. Shame stifled my breathing, and asthma resurfaced with the familiar stabbing in my chest. Through the haze of dizziness, sweaty palms, and skipping heartbeats, I tried to focus and set aside the shame I felt as the eyes of the courtroom were all upon me.

The pain of living with the horror of the revelation of sexual abuse in our home was debilitating. Wondering who all knew our story and what version they knew just magnified the pain. But it was an entirely different matter to be in a position of having the greatest sorrow of your life exploited in a court of law for the advantage of the one who caused all your pain. False accusations hurled at me in an attempt to gain the upper hand in a visitation lawsuit caused intense anxiety and suffering while I tried to hold on, help my children heal, and continue to home educate my children.

Shame from visitations by police and social services and the dreaded ringing of the doorbell invaded our privacy and put us all in shock. Did the neighbors see the police car pull up to our door? Then there were the never-ending appointments with counselors that sometimes inflicted even more pain—heartrending new revelations and endless tears that break a mother's heart in the middle of the night. I tried to make the counseling appointment experience a fun one—snacks for us all while we waited for our counseling—and mama gained weight. I wasn't the one on trial, but during the court proceedings that filled five years of my life, the other side attempted to use shame and slander about me to produce a favorable outcome for their client.

This is what public shaming does. It influences the crowd in an attempt to condemn the object of shame. But in the midst of that broken place, when I cried out from the rubble of shame covering me so deeply, a still small voice reminded me that my pain and shame in the courtroom was part of a mission to protect my children. Would I serve the Lord in this place? Would I count the suffering as a blessing if I achieved the objective of honoring their wishes and protecting them? Yes. Yes, I would.

Despite my innocence, the sting of shame reached me as I felt the disdain of some who believed the lies uttered by the opposing side. Did the truth really matter? I was shamed, either way. And so, I prayed. Right there in the middle of a deafening silence in the courtroom, I cried out to God, my Defender. Instead of despising the shame I felt so deeply, I asked Him to take it and to help me bear it. I asked Him for His perspective. I prayed for my children and begged God to grant favor. Suddenly, there in the middle of what seemed to be the worst days of my life, my obsession with the grief I felt over my suffering and shame was transformed. I did not care about the shame anymore. I realized that this place of scorn could otherwise become an altar of worship. Feeling the hatred and judgment all around me, I thought of my Savior. Didn't He choose such a place that I wanted to avoid? Where I had previously wondered how circumstances got me to this place and why God would allow such pain and injustice, such shame...I only felt gratitude. Gratitude that Jesus would do that for me. That He would willingly bear my shame even though He was not guilty. He did not complain when He bore my guilt and shame. Instead, He did it with joy. Could I do the same? Could I have joy despite my reputation being smeared by lies, my life being turned upside down? Yes. Because my life was hidden in Christ. My shame was Christ's shame. My victories were Christ's. To live is Christ, in the shame, pain, sorrows, and joys of life—all of it was for my Savior. If He allowed the shame in, He had a purpose that far exceeded my embarrassment. And God could receive glory from the ashes as I offered them up to Him.

Stumbling Blocks to Stopping Shame's Impact

As shame tries to wrap its tentacles around our minds and hearts, there will be many stumbling blocks to prevent us from overcoming the reach of shame. Most we will not even see. The forces of shame are so intertwined within our culture, seeing a way out is cloudy and difficult. The tactics for dealing with shame in the world can vary from desperately trying to conceal shame (as in the avoidance level of the shame spectrum) to brazenly being proud about our shame and flaunting it. (See the Levels of Shame on page 83.) If we don't laugh about shame we will cry about it. Stories of "the walk of shame" people take are deemed funny because the person's shame has been exposed. This hardened response comes from souls who don't know how to stop shame's reach in their lives. Boasting about shame will not rid us of its effect. The frustration with trying to eradicate shame externally is that we can try to clean up our shame reputation on the outside, only to find that shame is still reaching our souls. There is no escape just by dismissing it, rationalizing it, or proudly admitting it. No, the reach of shame is only contained when we examine it biblically and understand who we really are.

Stumbling Block 1: Guilt

Silencing the accusations of the enemy is hard to do because our own souls condemn us, too. But by filtering our guilt through the truth of God's Word, we recognize our guilt is not held against us and God has forgiven not just our sins but the guilt of our sins, too. We are guilty when we break God's law, but our guilt is not greater than God's sacrifice. Understanding the difference between condemnation and conviction is where guilt is given reign in our lives or put to death. Condemnation seems justified. It has truth mingled within. We know we aren't perfect. Accepting God's forgiveness is hard because we often come from a works-based faith. So, we accept the shame as penance. We think we must earn our forgiveness. Someone must pay for our guilt. And guilt is stubborn. We can try to dismiss it, but the accusations just keep coming. What then? This is where the biblical filter of truth, humility, and grace is critical. It is not the truth about our guilt that matters, but the truth about what God did to our guilt. He bore it all.

> ## God's definition of us always overrides man's.

Conviction, however, is liberating for those who understand it is a kindness that God would reveal our guilt. God exposes our shame to set us free, never to condemn us. When we respond to conviction with gratitude and ask God to cleanse us from our sin and shame, He is faithful to do so. Still, other stumbling blocks can try to impede the effectiveness of God's covering.

Stumbling Block 2: Doubt

Sometimes old habits die hard. We keep visiting shame that was covered by God, as if to offer retribution we deserve. Guilt, veiled as doubt, brings us back to the former guilt we let go of. We look at the reality around us, and there is still evidence of our guilt. Has it really been conquered? Yes. Our sovereign God, who is in complete control, has all authority to dismiss our sin and shame. All. Just like Jesus lovingly dismissed it from the adulterous woman, He looks into our eyes with perfect love and removes any hint of our former shame.

Stumbling Block 3: Lack of Self-Worth

Our lack of self-worth can also extend the reach of shame. We feel we deserve it even if we are not guilty. We are more willing to accept a negative definition for ourselves because our worth is tied to a faulty definition of who we are in Christ. Wrapped up in the here and now, we have forgotten where our worth really comes from. Our worth was never supposed to be tied to ourselves, our imperfections, or our achievements. We belong. We are image bearers. We *get* to be image bearers of the One and only Holy God!

Recently, one of my children asked God what the purpose was for her life. She was disappointed in her academic performance and poor time management and felt guilty. The Lord answered her, "You aren't here for you; you are here for me. It's not about you." This is difficult for us. We are inherently proud, yet lack self-worth, which seems like a conundrum. To think our lives are not about ourselves seems to feel like a slap in the face because we are often so man-centered. Our worth was communicated when the God who made us chose to rescue us by giving His life for ours. His perfection for our sins. Our greatest worth comes from living fully for God. When we understand who and whose we are, our worth is not a part of the equation as far as determining our shame.

Stumbling Block 4: Influence

The impact of the internet might be far reaching, but there is a much subtler impact working in our lives: the sting of being talked about behind our backs. Have you ever noticed when people in a group behave differently toward you? As if they were offended, but you are not aware of anything you have done. You notice it when you walk into a room and suddenly feel as if you missed something.

There is a distinct impression that someone has planted thoughts in the minds of those around you to influence them against you. Their behavior or countenance has changed. Unspoken but palpable, we feel incapable of affecting the power of influence. And why? Shame is powerful. People feel a need to respond to shame. We don't want any part of it. So, when someone is shamed behind their back, people want to disassociate with the shamed. Any attempt to try and call out the shaming is futile, because no one will admit to it. It is in the secret places that shame is bred. They can hardly define it, but there is shame lurking in the shadows, casting its spell on its participants—invisible and yet penetrating our minds and hearts. Unless.

We can be unaware of the influence of shame and let shame rule our lives unless we recognize shame's influence and stop its reach. Humans don't often realize the influence they are under. Taking captive thoughts and putting them through a biblical filter helps us to recognize the influences all around us. As we evaluate influences, we can choose to redeem our thoughts and let go of the lies shame breathes.

Removal of Shame Using a Biblical Mind-Set

Shame is a powerful tool of the enemy, distracting us from who we were created to be in Christ. Christ removed all of our shame and set us free. Sometimes, though, shame creeps back into our minds, so the mind is where we must war against the accusations of our soul. When we really understand how shame is operating, we can be liberated from its reach. Shame can only reach those who do not filter out shame's lies. We have to be well acquainted with God's

Word to be able to develop a biblical mind-set. The mind of Christ is not formed apart from God's Word. God loves us too much to leave us in that place of shame, but we have to seek Him through prayer and His Word to be set free.

Remember Your Identity

Shame is an accusation from the enemy on our very identity. But when we are falsely accused and shamed, we can remember who we are in Christ. As the apostle Paul was accused in a public setting, his defense was not focused on answering their foolish accusations, but on defining his identity.

> Up to this word they listened to him. Then they raised their voices and said, "Away with such a fellow from the earth! For he should not be allowed to live." And as they were shouting and throwing off their cloaks and flinging dust into the air, the tribune ordered him to be brought into the barracks, saying that he should be examined by flogging, to find out why they were shouting against him like this. But when they had stretched him out for the whips, Paul said to the centurion who was standing by, "Is it lawful for you to flog a man who is a Roman citizen and uncondemned?" When the centurion heard this, he went to the tribune and said to him, "What are you about to do? For this man is a Roman citizen." So the tribune came and said to him, "Tell me, are you a Roman citizen?" And he said, "Yes." The tribune answered, "I bought this citizenship for a large sum." Paul said, "But I am a citizen by birth." (Acts 22:22-28 ESV)

Paul was defending himself and testifying before people who became so angry with his testimony that they wanted to kill him.

They publicly shamed him and falsely accused him. As they laid him out and prepared to whip him, Paul reminded them of his citizenship and his identity. What a beautiful analogy this is for us. When we feel boxed in and defined by shame, we need to remember our identity and our citizenship. We are a citizen of heaven by birth; our identity in Christ means we can let go of shame. This requires discipline of the mind. We have to believe that the shame does not stick to us. We can choose not to allow shame to reach us. What others say about us does not matter. We no longer live; Christ lives in us. When we consider that Christ chose to be unpopular and chose to be mistreated, we know that we are in good company. There in our shame, Christ is with us, too. Our God will strengthen and enable us to rise above the overwhelming feeling of shame and dismiss it because of who we are in Christ. God's definition of us always overrides man's.

Embrace Humility

Pride makes shame's reach prolific in our lives. We don't know how to handle shame and our flesh freaks out at the notion that there is something deficient within us. But there always has been something deficient. In fact, at our worst, it seems there is nothing good in us at all. And it's true of all of us. (Check out Romans 3:23.) Isn't that freeing? For real. Being willing to admit our flaws sets us free to let Christ live through us instead. We make a mess of things down here and might even be responsible for shame in our lives. But we are not defined by our shame and having the humility to accept our part in shame does not mean we are defined by it. Rather, when we are able to accept the shame we caused, we can move on from it because of the forgiveness our God offers us.

Keep an Eye on Eternity

Shame's reach into our mind-set is magnified because we feel stuck in the here and now. We can't see the future and feel as if our shame will never end. Adopting the mind of Christ concerning our momentary struggles helps us to recognize that our lives are a vapor. Shame is temporary and what God has for us far surpasses anything this world could ever offer us. Having an eternal mind-set frees us from feeling trapped by time. Asking God to use our moments of shame for His glory puts the focus on eternity rather than on self.

Give Yourself Permission to Accept Forgiveness

How can shame be so powerful? *We let it be.* Shame *can* distort our perspective and *can* manifest itself in many ways. The cost of shame *can* be profound...or not. We get to choose how we let shame impact us. Not convinced? Shame will still hurt, but its reach is up to us. We have to acknowledge shame in our lives to be free from it. But acknowledging the painful areas of our lives is not the same as being defined by it. Permission is a two-way street. Do we give ourselves permission to accept God's forgiveness? Do we allow ourselves to let go of shame and embrace the freedom of being shame-free?

Redirect Your Focus

Shame's reach depends on what we focus on. The choice is up to *you and me.* Do we focus on the pain of our shame, or the One who delivered us through it all? Maybe the deliverance we hoped for would have been to have never encountered the demoralizing shame, but having walked through the deep waters and seeing our God part the waters and bring us through them, we are changed forever. No longer untouched by the painful side of life, but aware of an enabling God. That is, if we have given Him our shame and have let Him heal us. We defuse shame when we let go of the enemy's accusation, let go of bitterness, and adopt the mind-set of Christ. Christ endured the cross for the joy set before Him. When we have the joy God has for us set before us, we focus on His promises more than our circumstances.

Resist the Voice of Shame

The elephant in the room is our flesh. It propagates shame and tries to keep us earthly-minded. But we have been given an incredible gift in God's grace that enables us to choose to walk in the Spirit rather than the flesh. We can resist the flesh. This is such a simple truth but so hard in practice when the thoughts or shame just keep coming. When shame is overwhelming, we need to resist listening to its loud voice and resist accusation or distrust of God. Shame is a lie from the enemy. Hiding our shame from an all-knowing God won't work. Instead, we bring our shame to God because we know He chose to bear our shame to set us free. The high price He paid was not so we would remain in our sin and shame, but so we could rise above it all.

Start Fresh

Still sometimes, ya just have to "get out of Dodge." (That's French for "start over.") There is beauty in blooming where you are planted, but sometimes God just moves us on. Not to avoid the pain or the shame, but to get us out of our comfort zone and to kick the dust off and go where God has called us for the next season of life. The shame we leave behind might show up again where we are going, or perhaps there will be a new shame that we will encounter. But when we walk through our shame with God, the shame loses its power to condemn us and becomes a tool for our freedom instead.

Shame's Consequences

Gazing at Hagar's son, Ishamel, Sarah's chest pounded with the questions, Why couldn't I have birthed him? Why did God let me feel such shame? Tauntingly, Hagar rubbed her victory into Sarah's face like lemon juice over an open wound, boasting of her ability to bear a son even though she herself had not volunteered for such a task. Sarah let the shame of her infertility control her actions, which led her to try to take control of her destiny to avoid the shame that pierced her soul. Shame did not just reach Sarah in that moment. Her decisions made in shame impacted the rest of her life—far beyond the time when she felt trapped by shame. The consequences for taking matters into her own hands are still felt today. Modern-day enemies of God's people were formed because of shame. What if Sarah had trusted God in her shame? What if she had not chosen a shameful remedy to cure her shame? We may not be able to undo the reach of shame, but God can redeem it. And even the boy a slave woman bore was cared for because our loving God takes our shame and uses it to fulfill His purposes and demonstrate His unconditional love.

Change Your Perspective

What was it that we wanted from man? Praise? Our desire for man's approval can be idolatry. But some might say we just want acceptance. Christ warned us that we cannot serve both God and man. If the world loves us or if we love the world, we cannot love God, too. When we let go of man's praise and let go of the need for man's acceptance, we can reach them with the good news of the gospel instead of their shame reaching us. Man's opinions can seem endless, but they will eventually end. Being thoughtful about the impact of shame and seeing it through the eyes of grace, truth, and humility frees us to rise above shame. Shame Off You and me, friend.

Review and Reflection

Truth

Shame can't reach a forgiven soul. How does the truth set us free when it can condemn us as well? By praying and asking for wisdom, naming the shame and its lie, then searching God's Word for the truth to refute it. When we meditate on God's truth and choose to focus on our identity in Christ, we understand that God's salvation reaches further than shame ever could.

Humility

Shame does not define us, but we can be tutored by shame and then let it go by humbly receiving what the Holy Spirit prompts us to receive. We all fall short of God's perfect standard, but humility stops shame from condemning our souls.

Grace

Rather than seeing shame as an enemy, we can be grateful for the grace that shame brings to our lives. Grace to recognize our weaknesses and grace to forgive ourselves because God did, too. And when the shame is false, we can accept the grace of God to forgive others and let God's definition of us override man's.

Let's Recap

Unfortunately, accusations and shaming are not rare occurrences in our culture. In today's culture of pervasive social media, shame has a wide reach online, and it often takes the form of bullying. But we can stop shame's reach by understanding how it operates. Left alone, shame runs its course through a progression of levels—avoidance, self-righteousness, pride, and rebellion—and unless we can identify it, we can't defeat it, in ourselves or in the community at large. There are stumbling blocks that can keep us from stopping shame: guilt, doubt, self-worth, and influence. However, if we use these biblical mind-sets—remember our identity in Christ, embrace humility, keep an eye on eternity, accept our forgiveness, redirect our focus, change our perspective, and start fresh by relinquishing control and stepping out in faith—we can be victorious over shame.

Reflection Questions

1. How has shame impacted your life? How has it reached you?
2. How have you tried to stop shame's reach?
3. Who reached you the most with shame in your life? Why?

Name Your Shame—and Let It Go

DEVOTIONAL

Shades of Shame

May the arrogant be put to shame for wronging me without cause; but I will meditate on your precepts. —Psalm 119:78 (NIV)

There is a shame less obvious than that brought on by the intense stigma from severe circumstances. It is shame hidden in everyday life. There are many "shades" of shame in our lives, manifested in endless varying degrees. From embarrassment to deep shame, from guilt to condemnation. Others do it to us, but we also do it to ourselves. But there is a freedom in acknowledging that we aren't enough. It's OK to admit that we are imperfect. There is no shame in that. Why? Because Christ's perfection covers our imperfection. We will fall short. This keeps us humble—not shamed.

So, do you see shame sneaking into your life? You are not the only one, friend. So, what's the big deal? Why is it so important to deal with shame from everyday life? Because it holds us back from being all Christ created us to be. It distracts us and keeps us worrying about stuff that just does not matter. It makes us less effective for Christ, and it robs us of an abundant life that God has for us. Looking at shame through God's Word, I can choose to deal with and dismiss shame. We have to be able to recognize shame's impact to stop its reach.

A Prayer

Lord, thank You for taking our shame. Thank You for revealing our need for your grace and for exposing our shame, so we can be rid of it.

Part Two

Shame's Impact

CHAPTER SIX

Shame's Faces and Places

Recognizing Shame in Our Society

> *We can't escape the constant humiliation; shame is written across our faces.* —Psalm 44:15

> Shame lurks behind every corner when we look for honor and approval from life. —*Denise*

Being covered in yellow from a diaper blowout in the middle of a doctor's office.

Getting hit smack dab on the head by an egg hurled in your direction.

Peeing on somebody else on a swing. In fourth grade. In white jeans.

Tripping over the yellow brick road during a Wizard of Oz marching band show for homecoming. On national TV.

Slipping on oil in the grocery store and knocking a display of chocolate chips all over yourself. Death by chocolate.

Running at the end of a hiking trail, proclaiming victory,
then tripping and doing a face plant. In the mud.
Being erroneously arrested (twice).
Losing your baby.
Discovering sexual abuse in your home.

Oh no, these random occurrences did not happen to me. Nope. OK, yes, they all did. What I once wanted to hide no longer holds sway over me. Shame Off Me! The circumstances of life can be overwhelming and some of us are more accident prone than others, but shame rears its ugly head in unique ways in all of our lives. Being embarrassed by our circumstances does not make a lot of sense when we really think about it. Many times, we have no control over the circumstances that life sends our way. Why would we feel shame about them? Somewhere we believed the lie that we had to look perfect in every aspect of our lives. Mishaps and stigmas happen to other people, not to us, right? There is shame that we did not have our life together enough to avoid humbling things that happen in our lives, because everyone knows our flesh dislikes being humbled. But everyone who lives will experience shame at some point, whatever the cause. There may not be a way to avoid the shame that happens from circumstances in this life, but we can silence shame when we discover where it is hiding—and deal with it biblically.

Are you ready to see where shame has been stealing your joy and suppressing vibrant living?

Shame in Real Life

Shame hides in the random circumstances of life lurking within our perceived status in our culture. As we try to make our way in this world, shame hides in our homes, workplaces, and places of worship. It infiltrates our relationships and our minds. Those willing to investigate the "normal" way they interact with others and define themselves can debunk and replace former dysfunctional ways and embrace the abundant life Christ promises us instead.

Status

Our status in our relationships, families, workplaces, and places of worship can have a profound effect on the degree of shame we feel. All the situations of shame we face have one thing in common: fear of man. We all want to be esteemed. But when we elevate man's definition of us and then experience shame from others, we give them power that does not belong to them.

Our status in the surrounding culture is fickle. One moment we might feel appreciated. Another moment we might feel like we are the bane of someone else's existence. Toxic people can try to take us down in shame, but when we recognize their toxicity, we can let their poison go. I once had a sister in church inform me that I was her "sandpaper." How do you respond to that? Thank you? I guess she needed to get that off her chest, but the irony is that her disposition was often frumpy and displeasing. She was not the

> There is no shame on us for who we uniquely are. God gave us all the worth we will ever need.

picture of a contented person, so in my mind I figured the title she had given me probably fit her better. I also once had a brother in Christ say to me, "I don't like you," right before I went on stage to lead worship. "Well, I love you, brother" was the response the Holy Spirit gave me. Phew. But then there were the times when people sought to encourage me to tell me that they saw Christ in me, that I helped them to hold on one more day. Those times of encouragement are what I would prefer to remember, but sometimes the harsh words stick, don't they?

Where we get our status from determines our acceptance. If I need approval from everyone, I will have it from none. Shame lurks behind every corner when we look for honor and approval from life or from a fallen people. Sometimes we can try to get our worth or identity from our status. Others may revile their status. Some seek to acquire a certain status while others try to escape the one they have been born into. But our status doesn't define us any more than our vocation does. Status only limits those who choose to be defined by it.

When I chose to homeschool, I knew I would have to endure judgment and ridicule, even from close family members and friends. They felt shame over my choice, as if it affected them. They would tell me of their embarrassment when others would approach them and ask, "Why is she a homeschooler? Her kids will be un-socialized. Do they ever get out in public?" It was hard for years as I endured comment after comment and was expected to provide a defense for my choice to stay at home with my children and educate them myself. I reasoned that if godly men like John Wesley and some of our Founding Fathers were home educated, it was a good enough solution for me to educate the children God had given to me. Oh, and it was good enough for most of humankind before the public school system was established.

For the record, it wasn't that I liked being controversial, but it was a moment in my life where I followed my conviction even if it meant being mocked for it. I chose it because the Lord placed it upon my heart. I deeply wanted to instill character, integrity, and a passionate love for God and His Word in my children's hearts and felt that by teaching my children at home I could do that. I still choose it today and have for more than twenty-one years. God's evaluation of my obedience means more than what others may think.

Some statuses are worth sticking to even when others around us try to dissuade us. God may have moved us to a certain position to reach people in similar positions that we never could have reached had we avoided our status. Statuses in this world are meaningless unless they are in the center of God's will. Instead of trying to obtain a status for our pride, we can ask God where He wants to use us. God can do a lot with people who are willing to listen and stay in their status or calling for as long as He has them there.

Another thing about statuses is that they aren't static. Aiming to achieve a status that is approved by society is like aiming for a target in Jell-O. Statuses also fluctuate with the source we obtain that status from. One person or organization might readily receive us while another will not. Sometimes shame over our lack of status in one place simply is a means of God relocating or repositioning us to the status He has for us elsewhere. When we get a little comfortable, discomfort gets our attention.

What status have you wanted? Was it to be popular? pretty? rich? intelligent? successful? married? Shame or discontentment with our status in our God-given place in this life can also arise from craving someone else's status. Pursuing acceptance through our status is based upon our performance or ability to earn a certain place or position. That is temporary. There is no shame on us for who we uniquely are. God gave us all the worth we will ever need. And our status as a child of God is the most prized position of all. It lasts for an eternity. We can look to our Savior when we struggle with shame for our status in this life. The status our Savior chose was not exalted, though He is the most exalted. Christ chose a lower status to elevate ours. "He was despised and rejected by men; a man of sorrows, and acquainted with grief; and as one from whom men hide their faces he was despised, and we esteemed him not" (Isaiah 53:3 ESV).

What Christ accomplished by humbling Himself was the salvation of the world. When we seek to be elevated for our own glory, we miss the treasure that might be ours by humbling ourselves and seeking God's glory instead. Are we willing to let God choose our status in this life? He can do amazing things through a people yielded to Him.

Failure

Maybe shame has popped up in our lives because of mistakes or failures that have left a stain we feel can never be removed. Reminders and consequences from our failures keep us feeling shame, despite us no longer being in that place of shame. Failure is a part of life, but we desperately want to avoid it, because it defines our worth unfairly, as if there is no recovery from our errors in this life. But failure does not have to be an indictment. It can be a tool that humbles us and causes us to lean closer to the Lord, a bridge to growth rather than entrapment in our shame.

We all fail at something at some point in our lives. Trying to live as if we are not allowed to fail paralyzes us and causes us to live in fear of the propensity of shame we might encounter if we were to fail. The result? We might not even try to do something God has burning in our hearts because we just don't want to take the risk of failing. But, God has our back when we stumble and He uses our failures for our gain. God alone grants success and gives us favor and abilities to accomplish everything on earth that we do. And the success that God provides surpasses any success we could achieve in this world—God's rewards last for all eternity.

In the Culture

Y'all, we live in a shame-filled culture. If you have not seen it at work within our motivation for gaining a certain status, you might not so readily recognize shame's reach in culture. Shame is not so detectable because it is often so very subtle. We accept it. It has become a part of our way of life. From apologizing for ourselves for speaking in a conversation, to looking in the mirror repeatedly wondering if we look OK, or if our "fluff" (that's French for "fat") will embarrass us, shame is knocking on the door of our minds all day long. It whispers to our hearts and minds the lies that we breathe in. Why do we accept it? It is often quiet. Or maybe it has been there all along in the culture. Expectations set by man. Our lack of self-worth and not being well acquainted with truth deafens our ears to the real shame at hand. Our enemy is also planting thoughts and accusing our souls. Shame hides behind every door for those who look for purpose or acceptance in anything other than in Christ.

Growing up in a controlling environment, I felt shame for even asking to be considered. Shame was a tool of power used to cause us to be low maintenance and to be obedient. Kids were seen and not heard. I dared not ask if the car temperature could be changed. Shame on me for thinking I mattered. I carried that mentality with me into adulthood: I thought I was not worth having an opinion or being able to make a request. In my hurt, I recognized that I could go to the opposite extreme of wanting to make sure my children did not feel the same shame I did. Somewhere in the middle is being a good steward of all God has given us while still valuing people and their expectations, but not shaming them in their requests.

Comparison

Part of the reason shame has a hold on our culture is due to comparison. We look to others around us as being above, below, or beside us, rather than just viewing them as being unique in their own position. If we aren't careful, comparison can morph into jealousy and cause us to enter a cycle of shame. Comparison is a vicious cycle because there will always be someone greater or lesser than ourselves. Why not be thrilled for others when God is granting success in their lives? Developing a kingdom-minded mentality frees us from a scarcity mentality and the need to compare ourselves to others in an effort to gain worth.

Expectations

The expectations we have in this life can set us up for shame as well. During one of my pregnancies, I was absorbed with the necessity of keeping the precious life within me safe. But a foreboding sense lingered that something just was not right. One morning, I coughed and began to hemorrhage. As we rushed to the hospital, my heart clung to my status of being an expectant mama. I was both terrified and shamed at the thought of losing my child.

I lost my precious baby that day and felt engulfed in shame, as if I could have affected my new reality. But the Lord met me in such an amazing way that day and week. He provided a Christian nurse to take care of me while I was rushed to surgery. When I watched on the ultrasound as my baby's heartbeat slowed until it was no more, God comforted me. At a wedding two days later, when I had to sing a song with the lyrics "for every baby's beating heart," God used my pain to bring me to Him. He was there when advertisements for baby items kept coming in the mail. God met me with something I wasn't expecting at all. Hope and healing. Shame removed and replaced with an all-encompassing love. As I cried out to God and asked why He allowed this to happen, He gave me these words from the Psalms:

> Before I was afflicted I went astray, but now I obey your word. You are good, and what you do is good; teach me your decrees....It was good for me to be afflicted so that I might learn your decrees. The law from your mouth is more precious to me than thousands of pieces of silver and gold. Your hands made me and formed me; give me understanding to learn your commands. May those who fear you rejoice when they see me for I have put my hope in your word. I know, Lord, that your laws are righteous, and that in faithfulness you have afflicted me. (Psalm 119:67-68; 71-75 NIV)

On my knees looking up to heaven, tears streaming down my face, I never felt more loved than in that moment. While affliction was something I desperately wanted to avoid, there in my sorrow, I met my Savior in a deeper way and fellowshipped with Him as I considered His suffering. What had my expectations been? That did not matter as I considered what my Savior chose for me. God could take my expectations now. They belonged to Him. He replaced my shame and filled me with understanding. My loss was not about me, but about God redeeming my losses in this world and using them mysteriously for His glory. All the shame we encounter from the pain life sends our way can become a stepping stone of deliverance from that shame.

The Daily Grind

If it is not a traumatic event that fills us with shame over the expectations that are unfulfilled in this life, daily struggles can consume us with shame, too. All too often the struggle is real because it is all we ever knew. We learn shame by those around us in the way we interact with one another.

I pulled up to the fast-food restaurant in the dually truck with an engine that roared. All eyes were on me as I was conspicuously generating a substantial amount of noise pollution. And the air conditioner was malfunctioning that day in my current husband's beloved beast of a vehicle, so I was a red-hot mess. Suddenly rising within my heart was a panicked feeling I knew all too well. Shame. Again. People were annoyed at the sheer magnitude of volume from my truck. Screaming to try and be heard above the din of what sounded like the worst faulty muffler ever, I relented and turned the vehicle off. Was it impolite to have a loud vehicle? Evidently. Before driving the truck to a family member's

> Sometimes to be set free from the shame in our culture, we need reminders of our identity and God's salvation.

house, she asked me not to park the vehicle in front of her home. As I pulled in across the street from her home, she rushed out, hoping none of her neighbors would spy me with such a redneck truck. Busted. A neighbor walked by anyway. Shame. Why? Was my truck against the law? No. But perhaps it was against a societal norm of what would be considered a nice vehicle. Broken societal expectations. Guilty. And what was I feeling as I drove this truck around? Shame. What was a middle-aged woman doing driving such a thing? And then it happened. I captured those thoughts and realized I had learned those behaviors. My current husband, I like to call him my "Bo," was proud of this truck. It put hair on his chest. Who was I trying to please with the vehicle I drove? Society. Our culture might try to shame us, but when our citizenship is not of this earth, we recognize the deliverance from God even while we still live in a fallen world.

A Look at the Biblical Perspective

God removed the shame that His people felt while in Egypt. He can remove the shame we feel in our culture, too. Joshua records that God "rolled away" their shame: "And the Lord said to Joshua, Today the shame of Egypt has been rolled away from you. So that place was named Gilgal, to this day" (Joshua 5:9 BBE).

Gilgal. A place of worship, remembrance, repentance, reverence, and renewal. A place where God's people made a covenant with their God. A place of getting back to the basics in our walk with God. "So they all went to Gilgal, and in a solemn ceremony before the LORD they made Saul king. Then they offered peace offerings to the LORD, and Saul and all the Israelites were filled with joy"

(1 Samuel 11:15). A place where God encountered and spoke with His people, reaffirming His covenant with an object lesson they would not soon forget:

> When the entire nation was on the other side, the LORD told Joshua, "Select for yourselves twelve men from the people, one per tribe. Instruct them, 'Pick up twelve stones from the middle of the Jordan, from the very place where the priests stand firmly, and carry them over with you and put them in the place where you camp tonight.'" Joshua summoned the twelve men he had appointed from the Israelites, one per tribe. Joshua told them, "Go in front of the ark of the LORD your God to the middle of the Jordan. Each of you is to put a stone on his shoulder, according to the number of the Israelite tribes. The stones will be a reminder to you. When your children ask someday, 'Why are these stones important to you?' tell them how the water of the Jordan stopped flowing before the ark of the covenant of the LORD. When it crossed the Jordan, the water of the Jordan stopped flowing. These stones will be a lasting memorial for the Israelites." The Israelites did just as Joshua commanded. They picked up twelve stones, according to the number of the Israelite tribes, from the middle of the Jordan as the LORD had instructed Joshua. They carried them over with them to the camp and put them there. Joshua also set up twelve stones in the middle of the Jordan in the very place where the priests carrying the ark of the covenant stood. They remain there to this very day. (Joshua 4:1-9 NET)

The stones that were selected for their memorial were not pebbles or pet rocks. They were massive stones, heavy burdens for the men to carry. The memorial was going to leave a lasting impact as it would not wash away easily in the river but serve as an everlasting reminder of the covenant a Holy God made with His less-than-holy, shame-filled people. Sometimes to be set free from the shame in our culture, we need reminders. Big ones. Reminders of our identity and God's salvation. Sometimes we need a benchmark or a place we can come to and be brought back to our senses. Gilgal was that place for God's people.

It was at Gilgal that Abraham erected his first altar, and where God's people returned and offered sacrifices time and time again. God's people were led to repentance as Samuel administered justice in Gilgal. It was also there that Israel embraced shame when God's people resorted to idolatrous worship as recorded in the book of Hosea. The first Passover was held there as they entered the land of Canaan. It was to Gilgal that the ark containing the presence of God was returned, and where God's prophets Elijah and Elisha resided.

The very meaning of the word *Gilgal* is "rolling." God rolled the shame off His people—kind of like the stone was rolled away on the tomb that day when Christ overcame death and the grave. God completely removed our shame by His faithfulness. Not because we deserved or earned it, but because He wanted to set His people free. Even when it seems we cannot overcome the burden of shame contained in our culture, our God is able to roll shame off of us and renew His people. We just have to be willing to let go of the shame and adopt God's truth and acceptance instead.

Take Naomi. And Ruth.

Naomi (the one who told everyone to just call her Mara, short for bitter) felt covered in shame. Shame for God's lack of provision that forced her family to move to a foreign land. Shame for the death of her husband and her sons. And those daughters-in-law? Hardly someone she would want to bring back home with her. The judgment she would feel for bringing unbelieving daughters-in-law back to her home was yet another burden on top of everything else.

But that stubborn Ruth just would not let go of her commitment to Naomi, no matter how many times Naomi tried to shake her off. In the midst of the deep shame Naomi felt, she hoped that somehow God would still have a plan. As she journeyed back to her people when the famine had ended, she arrived right as the harvest was coming in.

What a beautiful entrance to the next scene, as God set the stage for restoration with a bountiful harvest! Sometimes if we are patient, right around the corner is a bigger blessing than we could have ever imagined, if we will just hold on to God and His promises. And that pesky daughter-in-law? She ended up ushering in a restoration of Naomi's honor and a new season of grace. Sometimes what we think is a source of shame becomes a blessing when we trust God with the outcome instead of doubting Him.

Part of how God rolls away the stone of shame in our lives is through revelation. As God exposes the myths we believe and reveals truth, we are set free. All the faces and places of shame woven in our culture might be loud, but they are not truth. Shame is propaganda. It is influence propagated by a culture intent on pleasing man. When we live for an Audience of One, the voices of shame all around us get quieter. We don't have the same goals or standards as the surrounding culture. The perspective of a world bent on living to please self will always end up in shame, but the Christian rises above that shame when our hearts are fixed on God's Word and standards instead.

Have you, like Naomi, gone through grief so great that you feel shame about it? Maybe you have wondered that if God allowed it into your life, then you really must have done something wrong. This kind of shame is once again formed from looking to man for favor. When we look to God in our shame, He is able to roll shame off us and restore honor all for His glory.

Review and Reflection

Truth

Even when shame is all around us, our God and His promises are greater.

Humility

The source of our shame is flawed, focusing on our weaknesses. In our weaknesses, we are strong. We don't have to be afraid of being exposed anymore. We never were enough, but our God is. When we trust God in our shame, He is able to remove it.

Grace

Whether the shame fits or not, God gives us grace to walk through it. He is faithful and will not leave us in our shame.

Let's Recap

The circumstances of life can be overwhelming or just frustrating, but shame rears its ugly head in unique ways in all of our lives. Being embarrassed by our circumstances—from slipping on the floor in the grocery store to something as horrendous as discovering sexual abuse in your home—doesn't make sense, though, because we have no control over these things. Yet we give circumstances that power. Shame lurks everywhere in our culture: in our social status (or lack of it); when we experience personal failure or make a mistake; within our cultural subcultures in which we hope to shine; in comparison and jealousy when we feel we fall short; or when our expectations are not met or cannot be met. Life is full of shame-inducing "opportunities," but sometimes what we think is a source of shame becomes a blessing when we trust God with the outcome.

Reflection Questions

1. Have you ever felt defined by your shame? Why? How did you handle it?
2. Do you believe that God can roll any shame you feel in your life off of you? Why or why not?
3. How do you think God can roll shame off you in your life?

Name Your Shame—and Let It Go

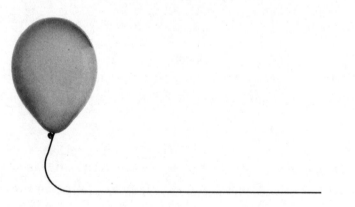

DEVOTIONAL

Overcoming Borrowed Shame

According to my earnest expectation and hope, that I will
not be put to shame in anything, but that with all boldness,
Christ will even now, as always, be exalted in my body,
whether by life or by death. —Philippians 1:20 (NASB)

Don't despise humble beginnings. Don't put your hope in man's praise. And don't let someone else's inhibitions become yours!

Choosing to live shame-free might carry a little sting every now and then. But don't let the pain of shame keep you in a culture of shame. It might mean people don't accept us in an attempt to manipulate or control us by their own prison of shame. We might not be popular with the "in" crowd. We might not be invited to some functions because we are "different." That's OK. Worshiping at that altar always leaves us empty. Being "OK" with who we are means we don't need anyone else's approval to validate our personhood, our clothing, or anything else that would supposedly contribute to our status.

Are we more concerned with fitting in or with being free from shame? I choose the latter. If Christ, who is Lord of all, was not ashamed to call us His own and to accept us, why would we allow someone else to shame us?

A Prayer

Lord, help me to let go of shame from others. May my heart's desire be to please you alone.

CHAPTER SEVEN

Shame's Cost

Evaluating the Role that Finances Play in Shame

> *The* LORD *makes poor and makes rich; he brings low and he exalts.* —1 Samuel 2:7 (ESV)

> When all we have belongs to Him and we are merely stewards, we do not own the shame that comes from not having all that we think we should have or the glory that comes from His blessing. —*Denise*

Standing at the checkout, I looked at the woman in front of me as the cashier announced matter-of-factly, "You do not have enough to pay for this order. Would you like to put some items back?" With a panicked expression, the customer began disassembling her purse, convinced she would find what she needed. "I had another twenty dollars in here. It must have dropped somewhere in the store. Can you have a manager ask if someone has found it?"

Oh, the dreaded moment when all eyes are on you and your need is evident to everyone. We don't want to ever admit that we would ever be lacking. It hurts. It is humbling. And inviting the manager over? I felt the pain of her shame within my own mind and body and wished I could disappear with her. "You cover her," the Holy Spirit whispered in my ear. "Pay what she is lacking." Without hesitation, I leaned over to the cashier and said, "I will pay what remains." Astonished, the woman who had been frantically trying to find the money she needed like she was in search of lost treasure, stopped suddenly and looked in my eyes. "You don't even know me. Why would you do that?" she asked in disbelief. "But Jesus knows you," I answered. The Holy Spirit gave me that one. Well, He gave it all to me, so I could help with her financial need, but more than that, with her spiritual need.

> The familiar comparison game occurs when we feel shame because we don't own what others do.

In that moment, time seemed to stand still. God was working in this precious woman right smack dab in the middle of Walmart. The woman began to weep, then grabbed me and hugged me, confessing how she had been far away from God and what this meant to her. "God sees you and loves you, friend," I told her as I hugged her back. The customers behind us were now smiling. "Revival on aisle nine," I said. This precious woman was overcome that a stranger would care. She wanted my information, so she could pay me back. "I would lose my blessing if I did that," I said. "This blessed me more than you know, to be used by God to help you in your time of need."

The truth was, I was not rolling in dough either, and I had also had my moments of shame at the checkout register that were in the not so distant past. One time, when my children and I went through a drive-through, the person announced over the speaker that my card was declined. Scrambling through every nook and cranny in our van, I hunted for any coin I could find that might add up to be enough. And the shame at counting penny after penny to that poor fast-food worker was intense. On another occasion, when Bo was out of work and I was struggling with asthma, I went to fill a prescription and left without the medication when I could not come up with the funds. Standing at that counter was humiliating as I tried to figure out a way to purchase the medication and my lungs struggled to gasp for air. My oldest son caught my tears that day and helped me calm my asthmatic flare up. When I was a single mom, there were many such times—times when I wanted to buy something for my children and could not afford it, when I could not afford for my children to participate in some activities, when I stood in line at the food bank to get food, and when friends offered me deer meat from their hunting trips to eat. These times of need left a lasting impression that still makes my eyes glisten with tears . . . tears remembering the pain of need and reflecting on how God met me at those places.

We have all likely been in a place when we wondered where the provision was going to come from. In those moments, we can be prone to question why God would allow us to feel such need. When we look in His Word, we see promises that His children will never go without. "I was young and now I am old, yet I have never seen the righteous forsaken or their children begging bread" (Psalm 37:25 NIV). Still, there are those times when the provision from God seems to run short. Where is God in that, and why do we feel shame for such times?

Our Identity Is Connected to Our Possessions

When our identity is tied to what we own, we are in a very vulnerable place where shame can paralyze us. In reality, we do not own anything. We are taking care of what God has entrusted to us. But in a culture where people have varying levels of provision, we can be tempted to define ourselves according to the provision we see in other people's lives. The familiar comparison game occurs when we think our status or worth is tied to our belongings and we feel shame because we don't own what others do.

Even if we think we are not participants in the shame and pride culture that is based on what we own, others around us can try to shame us still. Our "Green Beast" (this is the name we gave to our Chevy Astro van that had been the training vehicle for all of our children's driving lessons) was not the favored vehicle when our children needed a vehicle to drive. No siree. They would prefer to drive a nicer vehicle (even though they were a large part of the reason our van looked the way it did). Why? Shame. From whom? "Friends." Even kind church folk got in on the action of mocking our vehicles. We started to get a reputation for all of our humble vehicles. Every one of them was well worn, to put it politely. All had over two hundred thousand miles. And every one of them had been in a wreck of some sort. The jokes were persistent, and I confess I felt ashamed of our vehicles. As we would pull up to church, some of the passengers slid down in their seats to keep from being seen, while Bo would boldly wave at people as we passed by—he would even honk the horn. I am thankful my husband is so practical, though sometimes I confess I would have liked to have purchased a brand-new car. My husband wisely chose a vehicle that could be paid for without debt.

The embarrassment we felt for driving the Green Beast stemmed from seeking man's approval. We had to overcome the feeling that our status was wrapped up in what we drove. Driving the Green Beast could never take away our worth in God's eyes, but man, well, man is fickle, and our not so lovely van was not so highly esteemed in the eyes of man. For the record, Bo was grateful for it because we did not have to get it fixed all that often. He did not permit the shame others tried to cast our way to pressure us into getting a more expensive vehicle before we had to.

Testing

There are opportunities—blessings—that accrue when we find ourselves coming up short financially. There are things to learn. We are being tested. And there will be rewards. When we feel like what we have is not enough, there is an opportunity. God is testing our contentment in what He provides. Will we trust Him when His idea of provision looks different than ours? Are we willing to let go of our idea of what would be a blessing and hold on to God's? Being dependent upon God is humbling. We would like to be able to provide all that we want, according to our own standards, but God is teaching us patience and trust while we wait on Him. And sometimes what we thought we had to have as a necessity, we later realized was a luxury and not needed after all.

Giving

In our want, there is an opportunity to embrace our need rather than trying to placate it with material objects that never fulfill us. Feeling our own need can fuel us to meet the needs of others. Our need can spark generosity, cultivated by the compassion the Lord developed in us when we experienced lack in our own lives. Giving from our abundance or from a humbler place of need, we recognize that we are called by God to give. He did not call us to try and get our esteem from wealth. Or to load up our barns so we would feel safe. God is a giver. He gave His life for us. He left perfection to redeem us and purchase our souls. God chose to face the shame of being without, so we could gain something worth far more than temporary riches. Being in the world is difficult. We can get wrapped up in all of the financial goals and objectives of life so that we forget God's purposes in finances. Sure, God knows we have needs and He delights to meet those needs, but He also wants us to be about giving and not letting the things we own actually own us.

Sovereign Provision

What about when we are struggling greatly to make ends meet? The word *lack* assumes that God did not provide enough for us. When we do not have enough money for things we need, our first thought might be to wonder why God would let this hurt into our lives. Having unmet needs hurts. But perhaps this feeling of hurt, this shame we feel, is formed in comparison with others rather than in trusting God's sovereignty in His provision on our behalf. We don't understand God's ways. We think everyone should have the same portion, yet God's purposes run far deeper than equality and our earthly comfort.

Missionaries who travel to less fortunate areas of the world are often surprised to discover that native people who have so little are so happy. The entrapments of the Western world can also rob us of the joy found in life's simpler blessings. When all we have belongs to Him and we are merely stewards, we do not own the shame that comes from not having all that we think we should have or the glory that comes from His blessing. It is all from Him and for Him. We tend to rationalize that we are merely making our best effort to provide for our own families. While this is biblical, we are also called to notice the needs around us outside our immediate family and not scorn or judge or neglect those less fortunate. There is a greater purpose at work than mere provision: relationship. When we have needs, those needs make us come to our Provider to seek His help. When we seek the Provider in need and in times of blessing, we are not insecure or shamed when times of lack visit us. He is the same God during both times. God sees us in our need and longs to be our sufficiency. When we learn as Paul did, to be content whether in famine or in plenty, we discover the joy of trusting God at all times and claim a higher purpose than chasing after material provision and wealth.

Bo lost his job three times in the first five years of our marriage. We were in rocky times already with looming court and lawyer fees from my former marriage, challenges with a blended family, and health issues. And now job loss. This is going to sound funny, but when he came home and told me the news of his first job loss, I felt an unexplainable joy in my heart. "This is going to be an adventure," I told him. "God is going to meet our needs and has a purpose in this."

The first job loss was the longest and such a special time for me of learning to trust God. In sweet ways, He showed me that He noticed the little details of my needs and desires. When I missed some of the foods we used to buy, I told the Lord about it. What amazed me was how specific the things were that He provided. I missed coconut oil, feta cheese, cheese, and fresh fruit and vegetables. I did not tell a soul. But God had two people at church approach me, both saying God told them to buy coconut oil for me. Another friend brought feta cheese, cheese, fruits, and vegetables. We started with nothing at the beginning of that year, but God provided income for the next nine months. My oldest son knew that the Lord had revealed to me the duration of the job loss. "Mom, how long is it going to be? I know you know," he asked me pleadingly.

One thing after another happened to provide for our needs. A refund from our neighborhood association since they did not need our dues that year. A refund from our mortgage company. A vegetable garden that produced like no other year. Had we not gone through this time of need, we would not have appreciated God's provision. The embarrassment of unemployment was felt when we had to sign the children up for state-provided health care when Bo and I had no insurance of our own. But even in that shame, there were incredible examples showing how God took care of us. The shame from lack came from the fear of man. There was no shame when we realized God was orchestrating the details of our lives. He humbled the Israelites

> Our finances aren't a true measurement of our worth like our culture tries to convince us.

as He provided for them in the desert. Would we let God determine our provision and trust Him in our own desert? Yes.

Understanding Finances Biblically

Most of us have no idea how blessed we really are. While most of the middle class in the United States feel the struggle as they try to make ends meet and keep up with financial responsibilities, they likely have no idea that they are in the top 1 to 5 percent of wealth in the world. That's right. Even if you make $20,000 per year, you are within the top 4 percent of all people on earth. (You can see where you stand financially in the world at www.globalrichlist.com.) It might not feel like that to most of us because we compare and adjust our expectations according to the standard around us.

The fact that we have to be concerned about a budget can feel like we lack, but it is accountability—and a part of what God expects from His people. If everything were to come easily to us, we would not see our need of God and His provision. We might be tempted to think we own it all, when in reality we do not. The fact is, everything we have really belongs to God. Any shame connected to what we own is released when we consider it isn't ours in the first place. We are merely stewards. Sometimes recognizing the blessing of God in our lives helps us to be content with His provision. Being aware of our standing in the overall financial scheme of things is humbling because we do not realize how blessed we really are. This placement does not define us in any way but reveals how "little" in our eyes is "much" when viewed on a global scale, especially when it is seen through the eyes of God. And perhaps what we thought was lack is now seen as abundance. Provision is all about perspective and context. And God is our faithful Provider in it all.

Stewards

Some are given two talents, some five (Matthew 25:14-30). Some are given more possessions than they know what to do with, some are trying to figure out how they can meet the needs underneath their own roof. This whole thing about provision can feel like a burden, but God is watching to see if we will be faithful. Will we wisely try to increase what He has given, not just so we can be fat and happy, but so we can be faithful and prepared to give it away or allocate it to where He tells us to? I don't know about you, but sometimes I like to play it safe. In the parable of the talents, I can understand the heart of the servant who just kept his provision safe. It is a scary world. There are no guarantees. But legitimate shame came from that choice. He was not faithful to steward well what God had given. He kept it for himself. God wants us to take what He gives and watch Him multiply it as we invest it in the lives of others.

When I was a little girl, I remember wanting things so desperately, but I was unable to afford them. Even using quarters to play a few video games made my mom cry during a lean time because the money could have been used to pay for laundry expenses. Still, I vividly recall the hurt from wanting things I could not have. Wanting things is not the same as needing them, but to a little girl, a want felt like a need. I was too ashamed to ask for what I wanted. It is humbling to have to ask someone for something we know we cannot afford. We don't want to be in the position of being an object of pity or worse, being denied our want. And we certainly don't want to admit our need. But when we come before the One who owns absolutely everything in this world, He invites us to ask Him for anything without shame. God owns it all. All of it. And He chooses to share it with His fallen people. Those people, in turn, often complain about what they are given, thinking they deserve more. Knowing that God owns everything fills my heart with comfort. He has an abundance. He owns every cattle on a thousand hills. He owns the hills, too. He is able to meet our needs. Knowing His character—that He would care and consider our needs (and desires) even though we are undeserving—brings my heart to a place of humble gratitude, no longer the shame of a little girl who did not feel she could ask others for anything. The Owner of everything will not leave His people without. He is Holy—completely good—and loves us too much to do something like that.

Generosity

Generosity is a tricky thing. As Jesus said, the poor we will always have with us and the needs are all around us. What does it mean to be generous? Ironically, we can feel shamed into being generous, too. But God loves a cheerful giver who does not give under compulsion. Planning ahead and having a giving disposition as the Lord leads puts us in a position of being generous just like our Father is with us. Giving from our lack is the most impressive display of generosity. The poor widow outdid the wealthy in a familiar scene in Scripture:

> As Jesus looked up, he saw the rich putting their gifts into the temple treasury. He also saw a poor widow put in two very small copper coins. "Truly I tell you," he said, "this poor widow has put in more than all the others. All these people gave their gifts out of their wealth; but she out of her poverty put in all she had to live on." (Luke 21:1-4 NIV)

What must have been going through her heart as she gave all she had? Not just some, but the Bible says *all*. What faith and trust in God. What a heart of giving freely. She embodied true generosity that did not consider her own needs, but the needs of others above her own. We don't have to be afraid to be generous when we remember all we have was given to us in the first place. God will provide again. It is just who He is.

What Finances Aren't

Our finances aren't a true measurement of our worth like our culture tries to convince us. Finances aren't our savior either. In fact, finances can distract us and keep us from God. Ask any lottery winner that. Still, we tend to think that our troubles will dissipate if we could just have the provision we think we need. No more shame over not having the latest and greatest. No more bill collectors calling us. No more saying no when we want to say yes and bless those we love. Such provision can be a trap. God loves us too much to give us all we want. He wants our hearts to see provision as a necessary part of life, but not an idol. Finances come and go, but it is how we use God's provision that matters.

When Our Need Hurts

Sometimes the position of need we are in was brought upon us by someone else. We did not do anything to deserve such scarcity, but there is no way to avoid it. It is our lot. Blaming someone else or being angry with God will not help resolve our need. This is the position a widow found herself in in 2 Kings 4:1-7 (ESV):

Now the wife of one of the sons of the prophets cried to Elisha, "Your servant my husband is dead, and you know that your servant feared the LORD, but the creditor has come to take my two children to be his slaves." And Elisha said to her, "What shall I do for you? Tell me; what have you in the house?" And she said, "Your servant has nothing in the house except a jar of oil." Then he said, "Go outside, borrow vessels from all your neighbors, empty vessels and not too few. Then go in and shut the door behind yourself and your sons and pour into all these vessels. And when one is full, set it aside." So she went from him and shut the door behind herself and her sons. And as she poured they brought the vessels to her. When the vessels were full, she said to her son, "Bring me another vessel." And he said to her, "There is not another." Then the oil stopped flowing. She came and told the man of God, and he said, "Go, sell the oil and pay your debts, and you and your sons can live on the rest."

We don't know the widow's name, but God saw her. She did not just sit around and complain about her condition. She went to someone who could help her rather than let the injustice of slavery claim her children. Elisha did not just give her what she needed, he gave her a way to provide for herself. We have a part to play in provision, too. Man's part in provision is to work with what God has given.

Life felt intensely unfair as I tried to make ends meet as a new single mom and following the foreclosure on our home. Like the widow, it seemed like we had nothing and there was no way to provide for my family. I scrambled to try and earn an income to help us, while still home educating. I taught piano lessons, applied for a worship leader position, was hired, then there was a hiring freeze at that church. I was hired as a paralegal for an attorney who then ended up resigning to become a judge. It seemed like I kept running into dead ends. I began to sell things to make ends meet. I even sold my prized Korg Triton Extreme keyboard to my church. Even so, little by little, our situation began to grow more desperate. Did God see us? Would He provide? Yes—abundantly. Like the widow who saw God step in and provide out of seemingly nothing, God provided for my children and me, but it was not easy. Like Paul, we must learn to be content in plenty and in times of want. God is the same over both times. Oddly enough, I am now grateful for God allowing the lean times, because they produced a gratitude far beyond what I would have had if I had not experienced them. It is in our lack that we discover our God is sufficient for all of our needs and the contentment gained through such times is precious.

Review and Reflection

Truth
Our need could never be greater than God's abundance.

Humility
The need God allows in our lives is an opportunity for us to draw nearer to God and have Him meet our needs.

Grace
We are never forgotten in our need or in times of blessing. God reminds us that His grace is with us to be faithful stewards when we are in seasons of blessing and also with us to be content when we are in need.

Let's Recap
We don't want to ever admit we don't have enough money to go around. Or that our credit card has been declined. It hurts. It

is humbling. But that's because we tend to allow our identity to be connected to our possessions. The familiar comparison game occurs when we think our status or worth is tied to our belongings and we feel shame because we don't own what others do. But there are opportunities—blessings—that accrue when we find ourselves coming up short financially. There are things to learn from it, like the rewards of generosity toward others and in trusting God's sovereign provision. Most of us have no idea how blessed we really are, so it helps to look at finances—including our stewardship responsibilities and planning for charitable giving—through the biblical lens. It is in our lack that we discover our God is sufficient for all of our needs.

Reflection Questions

1. When have you felt shame over having a need? How did God meet that need?
2. Do you feel shame over what you own or don't own? What is the root of that shame?
3. Why do we never need to feel shame over what we own?

Name Your Shame—and Let It Go

DEVOTIONAL

Shame Off Our Lack

The rich and poor have this in common: The LORD *made them both.* —Proverbs 22:2

The boundaries of a budget—especially a lean one—can be a bummer. Ugh. So many times, I have felt the familiar stress from wondering if I had enough and trying to minimize our costs every way possible. And right there along with the mixed emotions about provision was shame. Shame over why we were constantly in need. Shame from feeling like I should do more for my children.

But the rich and the poor are the same in the eyes of God. In fact, it is the poor who are blessed by Jesus in His Sermon on the Mount. Riches are not always a blessing, contrary to this world's philosophy, but can be a distraction that can cause us to depend on things other than God for happiness. Acknowledging our need before God instead of trying to hide it creates an opportunity for God to move on our behalf. Experiencing a time of need helps us to appreciate God's provision and have our hearts stirred with compassion for others because we have been there before. And whatever God's provision is for us, whether it is a season of abundance or of need, God uses it all, and it is for His purposes and glory

A Prayer

Lord, thank You for being our Provider. Help us to trust in You when it seems we have been forgotten. May we also see the needs around us and be faithful to steward all You have given.

CHAPTER EIGHT

Shame's Past

Putting the Past in Its Place

My sin I acknowledged to you; my iniquity I did not hide. I said, "I will confess my transgressions to the LORD." And you forgave the guilt of my sin! —Psalm 32:5 (ISV)

Letting go of our ideal and accepting the real is a pathway to healing but it takes practice. *—Denise*

Letting the cat out of the box hurts. Really hurts. It seems getting a cat into a box hurts, too. Following yet another difficult pregnancy that caused me to develop pregnancy-induced asthma, I discovered that I was allergic to cats, and we had to get our cat out of the house as soon as possible. While getting the cat into a big box for a car trip to its new home, it scratched and clawed and fur flew everywhere. Sneezing continually, I longed for the moment when I could just let the cat out of the box and set it free in its new home. But we had to get it there first. Meanwhile, it kept trying to get out of the box. Proclaiming its presence with yowls I had never heard before, the cat caused stress to hit a new high in our van. It seems that cats can be pretty noisy in a box. So can the past. Noisily filling our minds with thoughts that plague us, we wish we could just let those thoughts out or reconcile them for once and for

> Hiding behind our fears will not remove shame off us.

all. But it is not so easily done. It hurts to have to face the pain from our past. We would rather bypass it than go through it. Like a claw reaching out from a box, it threatens to give us fresh wounds that only deepen the pain we recall from the past.

But keeping the past boxed up is not a solution. It will find a way out of the box when we least expect it, and if the shame from that past is not dealt with, we plunge deeper into shame and sign up for the continual cycle of shame.

Obstacles Keeping Us in Shame's Box

The past is the past. This too shall pass. Do not dwell on the past. All sage advice, but sometimes it is shame from the past that holds us back from being able to truly move forward in this life. We try to let bygones be bygones. We seek to forgive and forget, but the forgetting is not so easy when reminders of shame rise up as voices from the past to try and pull us back there. It is almost as if shame "knows" us. Kind of like being in a circle of people in our own hometown who have relegated us to a certain stereotype or label. There is no getting out of that box. Unless, of course, we discover the obstacles that keep us in shame's box from the past and remove them in Jesus's name.

Fear

Fear over the shame we might feel when we deal with the past also keeps us bound in shame. Our fears are often not grounded in reality, but even if they are realized and our past seems too great a burden to bear, we can learn to assess fear correctly and put it in its place, too. Fears loom large and bully us into submission. It takes courage to recognize that fear is not our taskmaster anymore. It does not have to be. Perfect love casts out all fear. We might not realize how much of a foothold we have given to fear. Asking God for wisdom and naming our fears one by one is foundational to removing the control fear has on us. Fear may have to be removed layer by layer from our life. So many fears may need to be addressed. Fear of man. Fear of pain. Fear of shame. Fear of consequences for dredging up what we wanted to stay hidden. The list goes on and on. Hiding behind our fears will not remove shame off us. Once we have named our fears, we have a choice. Which will we allow to rule us: fear or God's promises?

I used to live in fear of what God would allow in my life next. Then I realized I was imagining my future apart from His grace. His grace is sufficient for every burden we bear. We will not necessarily avoid pain, but our God will help us carry our burdens and strengthen us to walk through the doorway of fear and pain and overcome it all. Sometimes thinking our fears all the way through helps us to realize that our problems are not as big as we think they are. Like a small monster casting a large shadow, we can shrink our problems if we stop magnifying them and magnify our Savior instead.

Honestly, fear played a large role in my life. It reared its ugly head in every area, from worrying about safety of my children and loved ones to getting some kind of strange incurable disease. Fear of man was pervasive throughout, too. Funny thing is, the fear of things I told the Lord that I would like to avoid were allowed into my life. Robbery in the neighborhood? Check. Miscarriage? Check. Abuse in our home? Check. Divorce? Check. Flying on a plane with a wannabe terrorist? Check. A child with severe allergies or disease? Check. Health problems? Check. An insane court battle that went on and on? Check. And the list could truly go on and on. This little weak-kneed timid one has gone through some stuff, y'all. No doubt you have, too.

By the way, since you're curious about the wannabe terrorist on the plane ('cause I would be, too), we were on our way to adopt my youngest son from Russia. Did I mention that I was afraid of planes, too? Yep. I made a deal with the Lord that I would fly to Russia if He would give us safe passage. Me and my deals. Well, in the middle of the night, a man hauled off and punched the fella right behind us. Due to being terrified of flying, I had taken sleeping pills, so with drool down my chin, I lifted my

> Punishing ourselves with unforgiveness will not remove the shame by thinking it will "pay for it."

head in confusion, trying to figure out what was happening. The mayhem was resolved when a flight marshal detained the man at the back of the plane. Next to the bathroom in my aisle. Great. Guess where I now needed to go. "Go around," the Russian man said to me with a thick accent. He was not going to let me by. "OK, God. This is not funny. I need to have a meeting with you right now in the bathroom." All those months of trying to learn Russian, and let's just say it was not so helpful. "Iz Vinichee," I politely said. Blank stares. Whatever. I decided to go through anyway and apologize in broken Russian. Once in the restroom, I had a come-to-Jesus meeting. "Oh God, whatever You want me to do—if You want me to die over this ocean right now—I surrender my life over to You. This is not what I wanted, but I trust You, God." Yep, there was no recovery from my dramatic moment with God in the bathroom, but I did not care. Stepping out of the bathroom with all eyes on me, I brushed back my hair with attitude and made my way back to my seat. I overcame shame from what man thought and was set free that day . . . in part. There were many other layers of fear and shame that the Lord wanted to reveal and heal.

All the things I feared—many that came to fruition—no longer terrify me. In all these fears, I decided to trust God instead. I no longer live. Christ lives in me. He is enough no matter what I face. Does fear rise up again? Sure thing. Old habits die hard. But now I have a protocol. Fear may have a name, but it cannot stand up to the power of God, no matter how much shame it is clothed in.

Lack of Acceptance of Our New Reality

We often stay trapped in shame from our past because we just can't accept what really happened. Maybe it was a traumatic event that we keep stumbling over. We never wanted this testimony, but we don't realize God is crafting it all into our story for His glory. He uses it all. Letting go of our ideal and accepting the real is a pathway to healing but it takes practice. Instead of holding on to our dream as if we could make it come back alive, we have to choose to accept the death of *that* plan and *that* dream—and embrace (not just tolerate) our new normal. We might not like our new normal. We might long for a chance to make our past right again, but the opportunity is gone. And the plans and dreams God has waiting for us are far superior, anyway.

During a season of my life when our home was being foreclosed and everything was breaking that could break in my home and life, I wanted to go back to what I knew. Even if it hurt, I would find a way and still keep my children safe. The desolation of our lives hurt so bad I did not know how I could make it in this new territory. But God has a way of reaching us in those pits through creative means. While we are tempted to look back and wonder what in the world just happened, God is gently nudging us to keep moving forward. What we thought was a death and an end was, in fact, His mighty deliverance. In that empty, numb state, I cried out to God for healing from my past. I wished I had another story. I wished I could bury the shame that permeated my being. And then there was this song that I heard, and its words

> Our response to the past will define how we will live out this life.

spoke healing that helped me to let go of the past just a little. Sara Groves's song "Painting Pictures of Egypt" met me at a time when I was looking at *my* Egypt and wondering what God was up to. The closing lyrics from the chorus pierced my heart with my new reality: "But the places that used to fit me cannot hold the things I've learned." I could not keep pain from reaching me, could not pretend the things did not happen that did. I no longer fit within my former reality, but God could help me survive and even thrive in my new circumstances.

It wasn't returning to the past that would heal me. God's plans for me were far superior than my trying to cover up and hide the shame from my past. He wanted to use that place of pain to free me and others. Hiding the shame would not heal it but revealing the shame and dealing with it biblically would. God had lessons in the sorrows and heartache that would be wasted if they were just buried. What were once viewed as burdens I wished I could erase became treasures as the Lord drew me nearer to Himself and healed me from the shame of the past.

Learning to Forgive Ourselves

Sometimes we suffer from shame over the thought that we are culpable for misdeeds (sin) and pain from the past. Shame for our part in it. We rationalize and kick the matter over in our brains to try and remove any responsibility. Maybe the pain in the past was not largely our fault. Maybe it was. In either case, forgiveness needs to take place. Forgiving others and releasing bitterness removes residual shame just as much as forgiving ourselves does. God knew we needed a Savior. He knew we would have troubles in this world and He overcame them all for us. Still we struggle to forgive ourselves. Punishing ourselves with unforgiveness will not remove the shame by thinking it will "pay for it." Forgiveness plays an important part in our healing process. Without forgiveness, we stay bound in our shame. We can't break free because the counterparts to unforgiveness—such as bitterness, anger, or a victim mentality—hold us fast.

Bitterness

Bitterness is one step toward the unforgiveness trap. It rises from a sense of entitlement. We did not deserve the mess we got. Or the shame that our messes bring. The other person does not deserve forgiveness. We don't either. Failed expectations lead us down the winding path of bitterness, but there is a way out. Recognizing that the root of bitterness is formed from unmet expectations and disillusionment with God, we realize that when we become embittered, we are saying that God's plan for us was not enough. We deserved better. Ouch. We can choose to get better, not bitter, by remembering what we really deserved. God had mercy on us and died to save us. He loved us throughout. He died and rose again to give us resurrection life, where we can rise above bitterness and walk in His grace instead.

Anger

Related to bitterness, but down a pathway trodden with passionate stomps, is anger, yet another obstacle formed in unforgiveness. This is when bitterness becomes a demand. No longer just disillusioned, we refuse to accept our new normal and decide to become entrenched with anger toward God, other people, and ourselves. Being angry will not resolve the shame from our past; it will just cause it to fester. Anger is an accusation and an outcry from a broken heart that has given up hope and replaced it with cynicism.

Victim Mentality

We might not readily recognize our participation in victimhood, but it is a default position for mankind. It is simply easier to rationalize our shame away by claiming that we are the victim. I once knew a teenager who made the choice to allow bitterness and anger to define her. She always had a chip on her shoulder and was blind to the behavior she exhibited. She had suffered sorrow and a broken family, and she wanted everyone around her to know just how miserable she was. Her family tried to love her, but she would not receive it. She couldn't. It messed up her victimhood status and the identity she had embraced. She would not have her stories to tell and her enabling audience. But she missed out on an incredible plan God had for her while she held on to her victimhood. Sometimes our victimhood becomes a self-fulfilling prophecy. We let our warped view become our reality instead of reaching for healing and truth.

The victim mentality never fulfills us. It cannot heal us either. It is a vise grip attached to unforgiveness that keeps us bound in our past shame. We try to blame our circumstances on someone else and get used to the attention we receive for being a victim. We all suffer in this life. Having a cheery disposition in the midst of sorrow is not necessarily the prescription, but a change in perspective is. Our Savior chose to suffer. We will also. And in that suffering a funny thing happens. Suddenly, we become grateful when we have a taste of the suffering our Savior endured on our behalf. Grateful that our Savior suffered to heal us of our sin condition. The shame is off us in our suffering, too. Suffering is common to all. So is shame. It's what we do with shame in our lives that determines how far we let it reach us. Victimhood will define us in our shame, even as we try to place it on others. Rather, choose victory over victimhood. The reward we are gaining by surrendering to our God in the midst of suffering is eternal and priceless. It's also a lot more fun to be shame-free and walking in victory than to remain frozen in victimhood.

Does the Past Define Us?

The past may not define us; however, our response to the past will define how we will live out this life. The past shapes us. Will we walk in the abundant grace-filled life that Christ has for us, free of shame? Or will we allow ourselves to be hindered by the pain and burdens of this life—and let *them* define us? We are surrounded by a great cloud of witnesses who chose to rise above the shame of their past and let God use them in amazing ways. The Bible is replete with examples of people impacted by their past and how they overcame. King David is one such example.

When we look at the life of a man after God's own heart, we see someone who was God's first choice to be the king of Israel to replace Saul—but he was the last pick among men. And his brothers made sure that he knew his place too:

> But when David's oldest brother, Eliab, heard David talking to the men, he was angry. "What are you doing around here anyway?" he demanded. "What about those few sheep you're supposed to be taking care of? I know about your pride and deceit. You just want to see the battle!" "What have I done now?" David replied. "I was only asking a question!" (1 Samuel 17:28-29)

Ever have someone in your life who continually reminds you of how small you are? David was the runt of the litter. He knew it well. But He was faithful. Despite the shame of his low position as a shepherd, God elevated David to be the king of His people. While he might have suffered in his childhood, as an adult, David incurred shame at his own hands.

David could have had any woman he wanted, but he had to have Bathsheba—a married woman. And he chose to have her husband murdered, too. I don't know about you, but David's decision here wrecks me every time. When I consider that he was known to be a man after God's own heart, I realize that we are all just as capable of falling. Despite his guilt, David acknowledged his sins and repented when Nathan the prophet confronted him. And God forgave him. David kept the humility resulting from his sins but let go of the shame. Even so, David learned that past mistakes have a way of producing consequences. In all of David's trials, we see a heart of worship in one who drew near to God. His past, his present, and his future were in God's hands (Psalm 31:15). If God accepted him, then no shame in his past could take that away.

God has a way of making us face the past rather than avoiding it. He cares too much about our healing to let us live lives steeped in shame from the past. Moses is another example of someone who could have allowed the past to prevent him from being used mightily. When God called Moses back to Egypt to be his voice for his people, Moses did not want to go. It's understandable. He had murdered an Egyptian and fled. I totally get Moses trying to use excuses about a speech impediment that would prevent him from going on this excursion to let God's people go. I think I would've had a speech impediment, too, just from trembling at the thought of facing such formidable opposition. We all feel that way, don't we? No one wants to go back to a painful past, but we can't move forward if we don't go back. When I examined my own past when writing this book, I examined it through God's truth, and I am set free from the condemnation of my old story, set free to see my new story. Shame off me. And maybe my story can help heal and shape yours for God's glory, too. Shame Off You!

Don't let the past define you any longer. You don't have to be held back with regret or accusations against your soul that make you feel less than. God is able to take our past and turn it into a blessing for the future.

Review and Reflection

Truth
If God accepts us, then no shame in our past can take that away.

Humility
In humility, we consider the grace of God that spared us from things we are not even aware of.

Grace
God weaves together all that is allowed into our lives into a beautiful story for His glory.

Let's Recap
Does the past define us? With our hearts and minds filled with shame for a past misdeed or sorrow, we wish we could just put it behind us once and for all. But it is not so easily done. It hurts to have to face the pain from our past. There are obstacles, too, that stand in the way of releasing past shame: fear of more shame, for example, or lack of acceptance of our present reality. Sometimes we suffer from shame over the thought that we are culpable for the shame and pain from the past, shame for our part in it. Forgiveness plays an important part in our healing process: we can't seem to break free because the counterparts to unforgiveness—such as

bitterness, anger, or a victim mentality—hold us fast. In the end, we must recognize that the past does shape us, but it is our response to the past that defines how we will live out this life. God is able to take our past and turn it into a blessing for the future.

Reflection Questions

1. Is there something in your past that you need to let go of? Why do you hold onto it?
2. What takeaway from this chapter will help you let go of the shame from your past?
3. Do you feel like your past defines you? Why or why not?

Name Your Shame—and Let It Go

DEVOTIONAL

Shame Off Our Past

Those who look to him are radiant; their faces are never covered with shame. —Psalm 34:5 (NIV)

Waking up from a nightmare, my thoughts raced with memories from the past. I realized I was not in that place anymore, but I was trying to "fix" problems in my dream. Moments of the past, good and bad, still affect our present. However, we are not so different from the saints of old whose checkered pasts filled with pain and consequences of their actions or circumstances could have held them back. There was Paul, the murderer; David, the adulterer/murderer; Peter, the traitor; Abigail, an abused wife; and Ruth, a widow. Despite their pasts filled with pain, they rose above, and God did miraculous things through them. Consequences can result in a hardened heart toward God or can be used to draw us nearer to Him to overcome our past.

The same God Who enabled the saints can enable us, too. They did not allow the past to hold them back, and we don't have to either. The past is the past, but its reach is up to us. We can bravely face the past because our God was there. He is in the present and He is in the future with us, too. The past does not define us because Christ has given us His identity.

A Prayer

Lord, thank You for Your grace that Your mercies are new each and every morning. Help me to trust your hand when the past hurts and to look to the future with the hope You have for me.

CHAPTER NINE

Shame's Mind

Overcoming the Battles in Our Mind

> *We are destroying speculations and every lofty thing raised up against the knowledge of God, and we are taking every thought captive to the obedience of Christ.* —2 Corinthians 10:5 (NASB)

> At the heart of our relationships is this craving for acceptance, but our mind is where the battle takes place—whether or not we will silence shame or listen to it.
> —*Denise*

Walking into the bathroom, I could feel all eyes upon me. My mind raced with thoughts of wondering what they were thinking of me. To make matters worse, I had chocolate on my bum (white pants), was running late after missing a month of college due to getting mononucleosis, and was pretty sure I was going to bomb the exam I had just driven thirty minutes to take. On the way to class, my horn decided to stick and honk at the police officer as I was speeding by, which subsequently led to me getting pulled over and getting a ticket. Cookie crumbs on me and a dazed look, I am sure I gave that police officer a good laugh. This all happened on Good Luck Road. Really? It was not going to be a good luck day at all. But then, I had more citations on Good Luck Road than anywhere else. Go figure. My life.

As I stood there in the bathroom trying to figure out a solution to avoid the shame I felt for being such a mess, the truth is, all the people surrounding me had no idea I had just come through such an epic odyssey to make it to class. They also might not have even noticed the chocolate on my derrière had I not stood in the bathroom trying to scrub it off and then eventually tied a jacket around my waist for the characteristic look that told everyone around me that I must have had some sort of accident. No one—I mean no one—ties a jacket around their waist unless they have something to hide. OK, there are some who do it for fashion, but the rest of us do it out of desperation.

But still, we can manufacture or conjure up ideas and maybe even create the very scenario we are seeking to avoid without even realizing it. I let the fear of a chocolate stain on my pants lead me on an adventure that day. Walking to the other side of campus, I made my way to a less visited bathroom and took my pants off to scrub them in the sink. "Out, spot!" I felt like Lady Macbeth trying to scrub off sin's stain to no avail. There I stood with my precious

> **Sometimes in the midst of a shameful place, we are on the cusp of something great if we surrender to God's purposes and let Him work in our lives.**

jacket around my waist with no pants on when someone walked into the bathroom. Yep. This was likely more shameful than had I just endured a little chocolate stain with a jacket tied around my waist. "I can help you. We have a washing machine and dryer as well as costumes down in the drama department. I can take your pants and go get a costume for you to wear."

"Really? Oh, that would be so wonderful. Thank you so much!" So, this blondie here has been a trusting individual for most of her life. Maybe a little too trusting. There I stood in the bathroom waiting for what seemed like an eternity. With. No. Pants. On. Surely that person would not forget about me or run off with my pants, would she? In the end, the stranger finally came up with a Spanish costume for me to wear while I waited. Yep. Definitely not drawing attention to myself in this situation. In my desire to avoid the shame I thought I would encounter, I created a much more shameful experience for myself. And for what? Because I was afraid of what people would say about a little stain? Because I was embarrassed by what looked like poop on my white pants?

Embarrassment is on the shame spectrum. Whether we create shame (embarrassment) or not does not reduce its impact on us. Some shame we experience because others cast it upon us, but I would say a lot of shame we do to ourselves, and the fear of man is an impetus for it.

> At the heart of our relationships is this craving for acceptance, but our mind is where the battle takes place, whether or not we will silence shame or listen to it.

We Must Battle for Control of Our Own Mind

The mind is where the battles of this life all first take place. One would think that we could have better control of our mind—it's ours after all. But sometimes we grow weary and would rather give in. Discouraged from the warfare we encounter within our own selves, we face many invisible foes in pride, insecurities, fear, pressure, and temptation, to name a few. But those who want to have shame removed from their lives have got to stay in the fight to be able to experience the freedom of the Shame-Off-You life. Ready? Let's face these foes together.

Pride

Sometimes we waste so much time worrying about people seeing us in our less than glorifying moments. We have an image to uphold. We have to avoid shame at all costs to maintain that image. This is all vanity and pride. We waste so much mental energy trying to measure up to some invisible standard because we want to make a good impression—or we get caught up in that whole acceptance trap. In humility, we recognize that we were all a complete mess before Christ redeemed our souls. Christ covered our sins and shame, but still we feel a need to "dress up" who we are. What if we were to freely admit our weaknesses and boast in them, like Paul said. With no more need to try to measure up because we realize we never could on our own, we would seek to glorify God by boasting in our weaknesses, so people might see Christ's strength in us, instead:

> Three times I pleaded with the Lord to take it away from me.
> But he said to me, "My grace is sufficient for you, for my power
> is made perfect in weakness." Therefore I will boast all the more

gladly about my weaknesses, so that Christ's power may rest on me. That is why, for Christ's sake, I delight in weaknesses, in insults, in hardships, in persecutions, in difficulties. For when I am weak, then I am strong. (2 Corinthians 12:8-10 NIV)

This humility did not just happen. Paul was suffering from some sort of affliction, described as a thorn in his flesh. God uses suffering in profound ways in our lives if we let Him. We don't know if Paul felt shame from the thorn in his flesh, but it was apparent he felt pain from it. Paul, used by God to heal many, could not heal himself? Or God was not going to heal him? Sometimes we can feel shame when hard or painful things are allowed into our lives, as if we were better than that. The rain falls on the good and the bad and in God's perfect sovereignty, sometimes the rain hurts, but He is there with us in that affliction. Paul turned a moment when he realized God was going to allow the momentary suffering to stay—into a place of worship. More than that, he turned that weakness into a strength. Christ's power rested on Paul as he let go of pride and shame and took hold of God's promises. Sometimes in the midst of a shameful place, we are on the cusp of something great if we surrender to God's purposes and let Him work in our lives, rather than trying to "save face" or trying to figure it out. Rather than allowing his thoughts to obsess over his suffering or anyone's perspectives on it, Paul took those thoughts captive. What an example of choosing to override the pride that shame emanates from and putting on the humility that sets us free! When we are free to admit we have nothing good in us and are a mess, God can turn a place of shame into a blessing. Knowing the typical warfare that goes on in our minds, we can prohibit shame from infiltrating our thought life and instead choose to think on redemptive thoughts by the grace of God.

Desperation

Being in a place of need hurts. Not just because it is shameful to be the object of pity (due to pride) but also because deep inside we accept a lie that we are forgotten. We begin to think our needs are not seen by our God who loves us. We might even begin to feel shame that as representatives of Christ, God would allow us to walk through such shameful experiences. But it is what we do in our moments of desperation that defines us.

The story of the Shunammite woman whose young son died shows her choice to have faith. But she didn't just believe her son would be healed by Elisha; she put feet to her faith and went to find the prophet. Her desperation became fuel for healing, not defeat.

> She saddled the donkey, and she said to her servant, "Urge the animal on; do not slacken the pace for me unless I tell you." So she set out and came to the man of God at Mount Carmel. When the man of God saw her coming, he said to Gehazi his servant, "Look, there is the Shunammite. Run at once to meet her and say to her, 'Is all well with you? Is all well with your husband? Is all well with the child?'" And she answered, "All is well." And when she came to the mountain to the man of God, she caught hold of his feet. And Gehazi came to push her away. But the man of God said, "Leave her alone, for she is in bitter distress, and the LORD has hidden it from me and has not told me." (2 Kings 4:23-27 ESV)

The Shunammite woman demonstrated tremendous perseverance in the face of a desperate situation. What faith she had to not accept death's answer as final! She knew where to run in her desperation. We can do the same.

Presumptions

The battle in the mind is not always provoked by external circumstances. Sometimes we can concoct our own burdens. Trying to read the expressions on the faces around us can send us on a trail of vain imaginations that might have no foundation in reality whatsoever. And if they do, we can internalize that reality to our own detriment. What is it about the judgments of those around us that can affect us so? You guessed it: shame once again. At the heart of our relationships is this craving for acceptance, but our mind is where the battle takes place, whether or not we will silence shame or listen to it. Presuming what others think about us is rooted in pride. How could we know another person's heart? This is different from someone actively demonstrating displeasure with us. A straightforward confrontation isn't hard to understand. It's when we imagine or assume conflict or condemnation where none exists that we come face-to-face with shame.

Insecurity

There is something about feeling inferior to others around us that shakes our confidence, as if we were in a competition and had to prove our value by being better than everyone else in the room. When we feel we don't measure up to others, insecurity rears its ugly head (a form of shame) and cripples our ability to cope in an environment where it seems like we are on the bottom of a totem pole. But who said anyone else was *the* standard, anyway?

We are in a losing battle if we become enslaved to the opinion and acceptance of man. The pursuit of acceptance can become idolatry as we hunt for confidence outside ourselves. The irony is that it is likely our own minds tearing ourselves down more than others. Maybe we can convince the people around us to look at us differently. Maybe not. Maybe they are not even thinking of us at all. Even if we were to achieve the acceptance we desired, the very people who had withheld acceptance before could do so again. And then again, it might have been made up in our mind to begin with.

Influence

One of the stumbling blocks that lets shame reach us is also a key factor in the battle of the mind: influence. Ever sat in a group of people and one or two people are just plain ol' grumpy and impacting the tone of the whole room? They are negative and dream killers. Maybe even bashing other people. They spread shame by trashing people. We can feel shame when we are the recipient of their poison. If they are not stopped, their negativity could spread. And if it is not negativity they spread, it could be that they try to manipulate or control others, pitting them against one another. Simply put, we are talking about toxic people. Their tool of choice? Influencing others through shame. We can get sucked into their drama if we are not careful. We can even initiate it if we are not guarding our hearts, minds, and tongues.

How do we stay away from such negativism? We recognize it as a battle of the mind and choose not to "drink the Kool-Aid" by participating in that behavior or endorsing it. If we put on our spiritual spectacles, we can see the real matter at hand is spiritual. Responding in the Spirit rather than in the flesh helps reverse the curse of a negative attitude and a negative influence. Head games are at the root of a lot of giving and accepting of shame. People think they have dominance over others with power plays. How silly. Planting thoughts in the minds of people to influence their acceptance or rejection of others ultimately can hurt the people indulging in such behavior. Gossips and slanderers can be found out, and people awaken from the stupor they were in when they were "under the influence." We do not readily detect the infiltration in our minds caused by influences all around us. Negativity or shaming is interwoven within the subcultures we live and operate in, but we can begin to

> Shame is what gives peer pressure its power. No one wants to be shamed.

detect it if we know what to look for. Like Paul, we need to take captive our thoughts, but sometimes we need help recognizing those thoughts, too.

Anxiety

Another common battle we face is anxiety. Rather than feeling shame for being anxious, we can identify with our Savior, who also experienced anxiety in the Garden of Gethsemane to the point of sweating blood. Christ suffered in the flesh just as we do, yet he overcame all of the stumbling blocks we trip over through the word of God. With every temptation that affected him, he countered with the Word of God. We can, too.

During one of the many legal battles I experienced, I found myself waiting anxiously for my children to enter the courtroom. I could hardly breathe. I never wanted them to have to testify. Once again, I felt unable to protect them. I had to learn to trust that God would protect them. *But God.* Those two words have become like an anchor to me when I was tempted to look at the waves around me. I clung to His promises and believed my God had a bigger plan.

Earlier that year my former husband had won visitation rights *if* our children said they wanted to have visitation with him. They didn't. So we went onto the treadmill of counseling until either the children changed their mind or their father and his family relented and stopped suing. Our lives were miserable.

The anxiety that victims feel over being forced to do something they don't want to do is doubly shaming. But in that moment when it seemed like we had lost, when my children had to testify, God defended us. He empowered them mightily on the witness stand. The truth became evident in that courtroom and we were finally set free after a five-year-long court battle.

Like the anxiety Christ must have felt as His accusers pressed in and He knew they were coming to attack Him, I felt extreme anxiety that affected me physically, as well. Anxiety is not a lack of faith. But staying in anxiety allows it to rule our emotions and heart and shame us from being who God created us to be. When life causes us to feel anxious, we can examine the root of that anxiety and find that shame was lingering there, too. Concern over life's problems and people's perspectives creates anxiety, but God's Word can quell it.

Fear

The fear of man is one of the chief catalysts for shame. Man's perception of us can steal our joy if we let it, and cover us with shame. We have a choice with the thoughts we cultivate. Will they be formed in fear, doubting God's ability to help us overcome, or in a healthy confidence that does not need to rely on man or circumstances for honor?

Fear had dominated me throughout my years growing up and into adulthood while I was raising my children. I wanted to be safe.

Desperately wanted to keep my children safe. I couldn't. As I navigated single motherhood, noises in the dark of the night threatened to steal my peace. Two robberies took place in our neighborhood that shook my confidence. One night, following the first robbery, the Lord led me to pray against the intruder and for protection. I prayed until I could not stay awake any longer and drifted off to sleep at four o'clock in the morning. The next morning, a dear friend called and said the Lord woke her up at that same time to pray for me. She said God told her to pray against the intruder and for protection. I later learned a robbery had actually taken place across the street. Fear had me bound, but prayer freed me from its grip. Fear drowns us in a sea of worry, shaming us from living boldly and fearlessly. But God can enable us to rise up and overcome fear with His Word.

Peer Pressure

Shame is what gives peer pressure its power. No one wants to be shamed. No one. In a group setting, when everyone around us is mocking our choices, we either are swayed by their opinion or we decide to give in to another pressure: the gentle nudging of the Holy Spirit, who says we are enough, just as we are. The Holy Spirit does not define us by our performance or preference, but by our identity in Christ. We don't have to fit in with the world (we're not supposed to). We are accepted just as we are. This radical acceptance enables us to rise above peer pressure. God's grace helped me to turn down drugs, alcohol, and sex when I was exposed to these things in middle school. A child of multiple divorces living in a bad part of the neighborhood, I was surrounded by people pressuring me to join them. Something inside me feared God. I did not want to hurt Him. I thank God for that.

But there were other times in my life when peer pressure proved to be even more painful. Peer pressure from kids growing up was one thing, but the pressure I felt inside and outside of court caused me to doubt my way. I questioned my walk with God. I doubted all I had known about God's compassion and forgiveness. I let people define for me what I was hearing from God. Then the Lord spoke to me from His precious Word and set me free. God does not pressure us. The Holy Spirit does not create confusion or pressure us. The Holy Spirit draws us to truth. How sweet is that?

Temptation

The enemy is a master deceiver. He tempts us then blames and shames us for succumbing. Our own hearts can condemn us, too. Sometimes we do have legitimate shame for times when we caved to temptation, but we need not stay there. We all fall short of God's standards, but He offers forgiveness to crush our shame.

In the wake of the scandal that rocked our home, I felt a need to buy *things* to try to heal and distract us from our suffering. As my heart ached to heal my children's wounds, I was tempted to think that things could help ease the pain. I threw out our old beds and bought new furniture for the kids. My children and I had never been to the movies, I was not a member of a gym, we did not have video games or television, and we had never had a dog. We bought and did those things. And, they might have distracted us for a while, but it wasn't lasting. And, of course, there was the ensuing debt. Temptation lures us, then shames us for indulging the flesh. Like the other stumbling blocks, it can be overcome by finding and choosing what really heals our souls. And that is Christ alone.

Deceit

There is a deception spectrum that extends from a bold-faced lie to exaggeration to not even realizing we are deceiving others. But whether we know it or intend it, lying to circumvent shame is a mind battle we have to face. So is learning how to recognize when others deceive us. We have to choose to fight for truth and slay deceit, or it will destroy us. Walking in truth helps us to be able to recognize lies so we can rise above deception.

When I was in middle school, I walked home (two miles) for lunch one day because I had forgotten to bring mine. A friend came with me. When I could not get into our home, she tried to be helpful to find a way in but accidentally broke a window. I had never broken a window. I had never broken anything. I was always trying to be perfect. My friend begged me not to tell anyone what she had done, so when my parents came home and saw the broken window, I covered my friend's actions and said I didn't know anything about it. I was a rotten liar and it showed. As the questions continued, my friend's parents called with her confession. I had not broken the window, but I felt shame over lying about it and was relieved when the truth came out. Truth has a way of stopping shame in its tracks and healing our conscience.

Bitterness

Bitterness, too, is a force to be reckoned with in the walls of our mind. Formed from a place of discontent or unfulfilled expectations, bitterness warps our thinking and steals our joy and gratitude. Multiple times when I was driving to court, I would listen to Christian radio, cry out to God, and pray. During those drives I heard the song "Forgiveness" by Matthew West several times. God was calling me to forgive before I even made it to court. How? What did that look like when I knew what awaited me in the courtroom? The Lord pursued me to let go of bitterness. One day as I was crying out to God for understanding, I shouted, "Why are we suffering for his sin?" "I wasn't angry with you when I bore your sin" was the response. My loving Savior wanted to set me free from the trap of bitterness. We might not feel shame for bitterness initially, but it will sure cause us to feel shame when exposed. And the fruit of being able to forgive and at the same time be strong enough to no longer be controlled or manipulated is simply beautiful. Forgiveness and releasing bitterness does not mean we become a doormat or that we have to let people into our lives who present a potential danger. But it does mean that we have let go of ill feelings and can even pray for them. What grace of God! And the shame that is hurled in my direction does not mean it holds a place in my life anymore. It does not stick. Shame off me.

Mind-Set Is Everything

Our mind-set can be our ruin, especially when our minds are set in shame or negativity. It has been said that what we think on, we are. Scary thought. Until Christ. We can take our thoughts captive and redeem them by choosing to embrace God's grace rather than the harsh realities of shame in our lives.

This world is tough. We learn to develop thick skin and possibly a hardened, pessimistic, jaded heart to cope with all the struggles around us. But thick skin does not prevent shame from reaching our hearts and minds. We have to form disciplines with how we process thoughts and be aware of the thoughts that come through the gate of our mind.

Review and Reflection

Truth

God is the God of a sound mind. We do not have to accept old mind patterns or behaviors of shame. Christ makes all things new.

Humility

Seeing our weakness is the beginning of recovery. We might be weak in our minds, but our resident God is greater. He is able to help us when we admit our need and cry out for wisdom and insight.

Grace

No matter how enveloped we have let our mind be in shame, God's grace is greater!

Let's Recap

The mind is a powerful thing. And we can conjure up shame without even realizing it. We have got to battle for control of our own mind, lest it run away with us. Some of the types of battles we face are: pride (rather than trying to "save face" or trying to figure it out, we should let God work it out); desperation; presumption (we imagine or assume conflict or condemnation where none exists); insecurity (we become enslaved to the opinion and acceptance of man); influence; anxiety (which rules our emotions and prevents clear thought); fear (which drowns us in a sea of worry); peer pressure (it's hard to resist the pressure of a group); temptation; deceit; and bitterness. In the end, our mind-set, our attitude, our mental discipline, is everything.

Reflection Questions

1. What has been your biggest struggle in your thoughts?
2. How did you use God's Word to overcome shame in your life?
3. Why is a biblical worldview mind-set important to develop?

Name Your Shame—and Let It Go

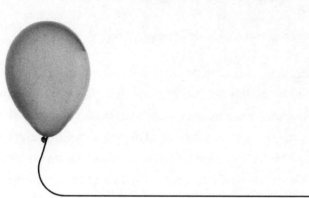

DEVOTIONAL

Shame Off Anxiety

Do not be anxious about anything, but in everything by
prayer and supplication with thanksgiving let your requests
be made known to God. —Philippians 4:6 (ESV)

We all struggle with how other people perceive us. The fear of being ashamed is about letting other people have the power to label us. Anxiety is a prison and it is one of the chief battles of the mind. It is unrealistic and traps its victims into being self-focused. Hindered by our fear of being seen, we forget about ministering to those around us. We are too busy being concerned about their view of us.

But others are not looking for us to be perfect. They are also wondering what we think of them. There is no shame for just being ourselves. Saying we are not enough is saying God did a poor job when He created us! By being who we were uniquely created to be, we live an authentic life that is superior to trying to project an image to satisfy others. Furthermore, when we accept humbling and even laugh at it, social anxiety starts to die. Looking to God for affirmation is far better than empty, temporal praise. And seeing ourselves through the lens of grace that God has for us sets us free from the warped lens man uses.

A Prayer

Lord, thank You for covering our sin and shame. Help us to walk in our identity that we have with You rather than trying to be an identity that fades away.

Part Three

Overcoming Shame

CHAPTER TEN

Confronting Shame

Exposing Shame's Identity and Embracing Yours Instead

I am not writing these things to shame you, but to warn you as my beloved children. —1 Corinthians 4:14

Our identity wasn't ever about us in the first place.
—Denise

We've come so far. We've examined how shame snuck into our lives, now, let's kick it to the curb. Shame is a taskmaster. It hunts us down and tries to get us to perpetually perform to meet some elusive standard. But now that we know how to biblically process shame, we just need to expose the last remaining stubborn shame representatives in our lives and eradicate them. Let's do this!

Shame defines us to the point that we forget who we are. Even when shame is not detected, we try to reach for the equivalent of fig leaves to cover the shame we feel. What's the big deal? Why worry about getting rid of the shame? Because shame's presence robs us of our true identity and steals the joy we can have by living free of shame. So, let's figure out who we are in light of all the shame that has gone on in our lives.

Shame Stole My Identity

We hear about it every day in the news—someone's identity was stolen. Scrambling to protect their accounts, people purchase protection so no one will take their identity. Yet all the while, they do not even recognize that their true identity has already been stolen. When shame gains a foothold in our lives, our identity is stripped away by degrees, leaving us feeling less than we were. Striving to achieve an identity in this world other than the one God intended will never leave us feeling fulfilled. That is an identity crisis. We were created for fellowship with God. Sin created a wedge in that relationship. And shame made sure that wedge stuck. What happened in the garden of Eden was a loss of who we truly were made to be: made in God's image.

Some of the methods by which we lost this identity seem good. Beneficial even. For example, trying to excel in this life is not a bad thing—unless we become enslaved to it for acceptance and, should we fail, find ourselves trying to stay ahead of the ensuing shame. Other ways we lose our God-given identity include performance, pretending, brokenness, and changes.

Performance

I did not realize how much shame made me perform to try to validate my existence. Whether it was competitions or trying to be the perfect daughter or wife or the perfect student, I hoped somehow that I would win the praise my soul hungered for. Maybe now I would be loved, I would reason, if I did my chores just right or I made people proud by accomplishing some big achievement. But it hurt deeply when all the effort was not recognized or praised. I did not realize that it was such a focus on self and a desperation in my heart that only God could heal. I could never perform well enough to get the acceptance my soul craved. But God all along freely gave that acceptance unconditionally to me.

> Our identity wasn't ever about us in the first place. All of our preoccupation with self keeps us bound by shame.

Shame tries to define us by our performance. We strive for excellence to feel significance, but when we fall short of our goals, shame chides us. And when we do obtain our goal? We falsely think that is our identity. Our performance in this life never could determine our worth or our identity. Identity is not tied to what we do or how well we do it, even though our culture feeds us the opposite message. But when we take all of God's gifts and develop them out of a place of an understood identity, as a child of the Creator, and we create alongside Him for God's glory and not our own, then shame is not tied to our performance whatsoever. And our great God just loves us, regardless of how well we perform.

Pretending

Shame told me that I needed to be like the people around me. If I dressed like them or spoke like them, liked what they liked, then I would be rid of shame. The only problem is, pretending does not quite convince our hearts. The momentary sense of belonging is a roller coaster ride of pain. Trying to anticipate who we should pretend to be next, trying to morph ourselves into whatever we think will elude shame is an effort spent in vain.

> If we are always looking for acceptance from others, we will always be searching for it. Acceptance comes from Christ and ourselves.

Once we've been deluded into shame's grip, we can also sometimes lose our identity by pretending the shame we feel is not there at all. We find ways of coping but don't realize as we go with the flow that we have gotten off track. We might even rationalize the shame we feel, making excuses for our less-than-abundant life as we accept our fake identity and try to do the best we can to navigate shame and keep it from defining us. But pretending just leaves us feeling hollow inside. When we admit that our identity has been transferred to a cheap counterfeit, we can begin to restore our identity in Christ again.

Brokenness

Maybe someone else's shame stole our identity. Or our lives are shattered and we struggle to put the pieces back together in the right order. Trying to grasp our new reality, we cannot seem to rise above the brokenness and doubt we will ever feel whole again. But we can get it back better than ever. It will require walking through the brokenness and the door of pain in order to be healed. And we will have to let go of our former identity in order to grab hold of our new identity.

No one volunteers for brokenness. No one wants someone else's shame to cover them. It is a weight too heavy to bear. The horrors of shame unexpectedly intruding into our life only magnifies the pain that shame brings. My children and I desperately wanted to escape the new labels we bore in the wake of our family tragedy. Anything to break free from the stigma. But the more we tried to hide it or not mention it, the larger it grew. It was not until we were able to look at the ugly fruit it produced in our lives that we could truly begin to heal. Brokenness might have temporarily stolen our identity, but it can also be a beautiful tool God uses to make us better than we were before. We would not have wanted to encounter brokenness, but we are forever changed by it and did not even see our need of that change.

Changes

Life throws us curve balls, sometimes at a frenetic pace. Our identity is stolen by all of the distractions that prevent us from being who we were made to be. We try to measure up to our new normal and transform into what we think we need to be in our new circumstances. The roles we play in the many stages of life require us to change. Our identity changes radically when we become parents, for instance. But our identity cannot be solely tied to that role. That is but one facet of who we are. Sometimes identifying solely in one function we perform causes us to lose our full identity. As children of God, that is our identity, and all we do flows from that. In and out of change, one thing remains the same: we are hidden in Christ and our value never changes, no matter what we endure in this life.

Our God-Given Identity Awaits

Even when we're lost or hiding, our God-given identity is waiting, dormant. And our identity can be restored again. Our identity wasn't ever about us in the first place. All of our preoccupation with self keeps us bound by shame while we do mental gymnastics as we encounter shame in its many forms and try to be enough.

So much effort spent trying to define our identity through our vocation, our achievements, our status! It all means nothing in light of who we truly are. We are His. Our true identity is in Christ. Hidden in Him. When we embrace our hidden identity, we are no longer bound by any of the identities we thought we had before.

Let this radical truth free you. We can stop pretending, worrying, and striving to claim an identity that's not our real identity in the first place and will never fulfill us. Having our identity in Christ helps us to face shame and truly deal with it. We don't have to hide shame—it does not define us.

A New Identity

When we understand who we really are, we don't waste time playing in the mud in an identity that is not our own. We are no longer haunted by past identities that try to accuse us or define us and bind us in shame. We are dead to our former identity. We say no to the past and embrace the present and future of who we are as redeemed and accepted in His sight. All the former stumbling blocks that keep us from seeing our true identity in Christ can now be seen for what they were: distractions from our true calling in Christ. We are accepted, chosen, victorious, complete. We are celebrated and loved.

Accepted

Rejection has plagued me for most of my life. Without realizing it, I worshiped at the altar of acceptance and agonized over all of the people who rejected me. Surely, I could be good enough. Maybe I could perform well enough or achieve something great in this life to finally have the endorsement or acceptance I longed for. I did not realize how much power I was giving to people by needing their acceptance to validate who I was.

When I was in high school, I auditioned, playing euphonium, for various music competitions. I made All-State my junior and senior years, but my senior year topped it all off—first place in the state of Maryland and in All-Eastern. Playing at All-State paved the way for a full scholarship at the University of Maryland. But acceptance was elusive, and even these accomplishments could not give me the acceptance I really longed for. (I had struggled to feel accepted—a product of multiple divorces in the various households I lived in while growing up and moving from school to school.) No matter how much I sought to achieve, it felt like it was never enough.

The need for acceptance is even trickier to navigate in such a public, connected, social media world. Putting ourselves out there for public opinion, we have to know who we are and not look to others to define us. This elusive pursuit of acceptance is once again shame calling our name.

The praise of people cannot fill the hole we have in our soul.

Other people have their hurts, too, and might be hindered from being able to meet our needs. Ultimately, achievements cannot give us the acceptance we long for. They eventually are forgotten. If we are always looking for acceptance from others, we will always be searching for it unless we know where to look. Acceptance comes from Christ and ourselves. Accepting ourselves for who we are in Christ sets us free to finally be who we were created to be.

However, walking in this new identity takes practice. As Paul discusses in Romans 6 and 8, our old man or old identity continues to knock on our door, trying to convince us that we are still that former identity. With my identity no longer in that place of being defined by other's acceptance, I now know that I am completely accepted by my Father in Heaven. His authority is highest, and if He says I'm precious and accepted, then no one can take that away . . . unless I let them.

Chosen

Sometimes shame can prevent us from receiving this acceptance from Christ. We don't understand why we would be chosen, given the messes that we are. It is hard for us to receive this acceptance. We see our flaws and let shame silence us. We might accept the fact that God chose us, but we wonder why.

Paul knew his shortcomings and that he was chief among sinners, but he did not stay there. His former identity as a murderer of God's people did not hold him back from being chosen and used by God. In fact, it qualified him. Our weaknesses and our former shame can serve to humble us and produce in us an explosive gratitude for God's amazing grace and be the very foundation God uses for us to serve Him. Scars from past sins and pains are shaped to be a part of the incredible purposes of God. God chose Paul, who vehemently persecuted the early church, to become a critical part of it. Paul said, "For I am the least of the apostles and do not even deserve to be called an apostle, because I persecuted the church of God. But by the grace of God I am what I am, and his grace to me was not without effect. No, I worked harder than all of them—yet not I, but the grace of God that was with me" (1 Corinthians 15:9-10).

Paul was chosen not by his deeds, but by God's irrevocable calling and choosing. He wrote thirteen of the epistles in the New Testament and passionately preached of God's salvation to the point of imprisonment and death. And so God chooses us, each with our own former identities and weaknesses, to glorify Himself. It seems so foolish to the world that God would choose misfits to assemble a motley crew of people He labels with their new identity, "Christians," but God delights in taking the broken, the hurting, the abused and rejected, shaping them into healed, saved vessels to be used by our Holy, Almighty God.

When I think of being chosen, I recall the dread of being picked or not picked for teams on the playground when I was growing up. All those times I was picked last? They don't faze me anymore. Our God picks us all first. How does He do that? He picked us before the foundations of the world. And He chose us to be blameless—shameless! Ephesians 1:4 says, "For he chose us in him before the creation of the world to be holy and blameless in his sight." This Scripture makes me dance for joy. God picked me. He picked you. He chose us to be blameless. He set His love on us and planned a way that He could remove the shame this world casts in our direction.

Celebrated and Loved

I wonder, still, how much Paul's past shaped what he did. Did he ever witness to someone he had threatened before? God has a way of bringing up our former moments of pain to heal us more deeply. God cherishes us and adores us. So much so, that He gave His life for us and paid for our shortcomings just as He did for Paul's.

This truth rang loudly for me one time while giving a worship concert. Standing in front of the crowd preparing to lead worship from inside a trailer with the rain pounding, I prayed and took a deep breath to sing. God had a sense of humor calling me to be a worship leader. My shy personality did not lend itself to speaking in front of people, and after all, supposedly the number one fear is public speaking. Double trouble. I wept before the first concert I ever gave. Why me, God? Why would you want to use me in this way? There are others so much more talented than I am. Kind of reminds me of some other people I know—Moses and Jeremiah. Both were called to be mouthpieces for the Lord and both said they could not speak well. Excuses, excuses. But God chooses the weak things of this world to glorify Himself.

> Our identity was never meant to be about us, but about being an image bearer of the glory of God.

As I stood in front of this group of people, my heart desperately wanted to minister to them, but I needed to get out of the way. I needed to put away my insecurities that told me I was not good enough and my fears that they would not like me. I wonder if Paul felt the same way. But from our weaknesses, God is strong.

Standing in front of a group of people is such a humbling thing. If we look to them for acceptance and praise, we miss the point of why we do what we do. As I poured out my heart in worship, suddenly someone from the audience shouted, "We love you, Denise!" It is hard to describe what that statement did to me in that moment. People often think that performers or leaders are self-assured or prideful. The opposite is often true. It is humbling to be so vulnerable to offer insights the Lord has given to us through song or word for others to evaluate. But in that moment, I was shocked someone would so boldly step out and encourage me. Loved. I was loved, and God used me to encourage someone who, in turn, sought to encourage me.

Most of my life I had not considered myself as worthy of love or acceptance. It was enough to be tolerated. But when we have accepted the label of being tolerated, and feel like we are a burden to others, we are forgetting part of our identity in Christ, which says we are celebrated. Our identity in Christ tells us that He delights in us! Ephesians 1:4-5 says, "*In love* he predestined us for adoption to sonship through Jesus Christ, in accordance with his *pleasure and will*" (my emphasis). God was intentional in choosing us. And He chose us with pleasure. Like that moment when someone shouted out their love for me at the concert, God is shouting to our souls, to the whole world, "I love you and delight in you!"

Victorious

Maybe we have accepted this incredible gift of Christ's identity, but we thought it was supposed to look different. Kind of like a completely victorious experience every day. But that depends on how we define victory. If we still need some convincing about what this new identity in Christ looks like, once again we look to Paul. In the letter to the Romans, we see Paul agonizing over his inability to be consistent in His walk with God, walking in the victory that Christ has for us:

> I don't really understand myself, for I want to do what is right, but I don't do it. Instead, I do what I hate. But if I know that what I am doing is wrong, this shows that I agree that the law is good. So I am not the one doing wrong; it is sin living in me that does it. And I know that nothing good lives in me, that is, in my sinful nature. I want to do what is right, but I can't. I want to do what is good, but I don't. I don't want to do what is wrong, but I do it anyway. But if I do what I don't want to do, I am not really the one doing wrong; it is sin living in me that does it. I have discovered this principle of life—that when I want to do what is right, I inevitably do what is wrong. I love God's law with all my heart. But there is another power within me that is at war with my mind. This power makes me a slave to the sin that is still within me. Oh, what a miserable person I am! Who will free me from this life that is dominated by sin and death? Thank God! The answer is in Jesus Christ our Lord. So you see how it is: In my mind I really want to obey God's law, but because of my sinful nature I am a slave to sin. So now there is no condemnation for those who belong to Christ Jesus. And because you belong to him, the power of the life-giving Spirit has freed you from the power of sin that leads to death. (7:15–8:2)

Wait a minute! This is Paul we are talking about here—blinded on the road to Damascus, miraculously healed, faithful apostle—

and he struggles with walking in victory? What is this identity in Christ supposed to look like anyway? Paul recognized both identities at work. On the one hand, his new identity in Christ had power to overcome. On the other hand, his former identity was still trying to pull him back to what he was. Paul is not admitting defeat in this chapter though. He was acknowledging the struggle, but he stayed in the fight. Maybe we thought that having our identity in Christ would mean no more struggles. We can pick up shame again because we fall short even as a Christian. The last two verses help us in this regard because we belong to Christ, we are free. It does not mean we will not still have to struggle in our minds and our flesh, but we are under no condemnation of shame any more.

Fully knowing we are weak and incapable of this great gift of identity in Christ, we accept it nonetheless and are made strong. We have the victory in Christ because Christ is victorious and we are called by His Name. We never could have had the victory on our own anyway. That's why we need a Savior.

Image-Bearers

What is the purpose of identifying with Christ? Obviously, we need salvation. Apart from Christ being our identity, our own identities are fallen. But if we all belong to Christ's identity, how are we different than one another? Each one of us is uniquely made and so each one of us can reveal the identity of Christ to the world in our own unique way. The enemy wants to keep us distracted from our true identity, because there is nothing more powerful than a soul surrendered to the identity of Christ. Shame is effective at causing us to forget our identity. But when we rise above the shame, we no longer need to worry about our own image and seek to be image-bearers of Christ, letting Christ live in us as we seek to imitate the example He set for us, only by His grace and strength.

We Are Complete

Our identity in Christ is complete even though we will see our weaknesses and our old identities trying to shame us, popping up from time to time. Acknowledging our shortcomings like Paul did, we don't have to struggle with feeling like we lack anymore. Christ has made us complete in Him! Colossians 2:9-10 says, "For in Christ lives all the fullness of God in a human body. So you also are complete through your union with Christ, who is the head over every ruler and authority." I have wasted so much time answering to all of the distracting voices of shame accusing me about my incompleteness in Christ. Maybe you have, too. Here's just a few of the shadows shame cast on me and how I exposed and eradicated them in my new identity in Christ.

Unpopularity

I have had my share of experiences in which people just didn't like me. You know the kind of people I am talking about: they go behind your back and try to defame you. You feel like rolling in the dirt and eating worms. Well, not really, but you feel less than. Can't say I love those moments. Funny thing, even though there is likely no validity to the shame, when we acquiesce to feeling unpopular, we become a slave to man's opinion. Running around to make sure we are not mischaracterized so people will like us is no way to live. We confront this shame by embracing who we are in Christ instead of man's fickle opinion. Putting on the truth of who I am helps me to recognize the lie behind the shame, which tells me that I am inferior. There is such freedom in being totally OK with not being enough. It is no longer an accusation—I know I'm not enough. But Christ paid it all and redeemed me anyway.

Perfectionism

Type-A people will totally get this. Never being able to complete a to-do list drives me crazy. And sticking to a diet for longer than an hour? Yep. I forget I am on a diet within minutes, especially if someone mentions chocolate. Trying to be all things to all people and doing everything well is probably still one of my biggest "shamers." It does not feel like shame, but if I were to try stopping all that I do, what would I feel? Guilt and shame. I would not have classified myself as a perfectionist because I am chill about giving myself grace when I fall short and definitely give others grace. But perfectionism isn't just about being perfect. It can be about being driven toward goals to the point where we don't know how to stop. Shame always cries out, "it is not enough!" I confronted this behavior by recognizing all I do is for the King of kings and He is OK with any progress. It does not have to look like anything I think it should. As long as I am willing to leave the results up to Him, then perfectionism loses its sting.

Underdog

I grew up as a shy, careful, little squinty-eyed girl ('cuz my baby blues are too sensitive to the sunlight), and being the last one picked on the team again and again got old. I got it. I was awkward and not exactly an athlete. But I loved baseball and thought softball must be in my genes since baseball skills ran in the family. Not so much.

When the ball was hit to outfield where I was looking down at the ground because the sun was too bright, a sudden surge of panic caused me to look up and contemplate actually making the catch and saving the day. Nope. I was afraid of the ball instead. And then there was dodgeball. I was always the slowest moving and most popular target. Then basketball. I had good aim. But taking the ball from me was like taking candy from a baby. You get the picture. I was the underdog and people always wanted to beat me up. What was up with that? I was just a shy, nice kid. But even as an adult, there have still been those times when people have purposely tried to brand me as an underdog. How do we tackle that feeling? I learned to laugh at myself and be OK with the things in which I don't excel. Boasting in my low position and in my weaknesses gave me strength I did not expect and glorified God. He alone is my strength. Funny thing—I am not such a bad athlete now. But I could not care less, because that is not where my identity comes from.

Insecurity

Leaning sideways, I carried my euphonium, aware of the callouses throbbing as I coached myself through the rest of the long walk home. Why, at four foot ten I picked this instrument, I will never know. Somehow, it made me feel safe. I could play for others but not be seen. I would put the music stand just high enough to block my face. Safe. No one's opinion or perception was viewable, and they could not see me while I puffed my cheeks. I spent most of my life trying to be safe, only to have my world fall apart when I least expected it. Carefully not stepping on cracks on the sidewalk (I was one of *those* people), staying away from bad things while growing up, always trying to keep myself and loved ones from being hurt.

Little by little as all my safe world collapsed, I realized my security had been in the wrong place. Suddenly aware of the bondage that the pursuit of safety had on me, I confronted the stifling shame of insecurity and professed that whatever God allowed into my life, it was no longer my life, but His. He was my security; having a perfect life was not possible and was no longer my goal. We expose the lies of shame when we realize we don't have to live by them anymore. Phew! What a burden those former identities are. The pressure is off as we live for One. The more we walk in the Spirit and resist the flesh, the more the shame falls off of us and is unrecognizable.

Review and Reflection

Truth

In Christ, our identity is complete. There is nothing more we could add to improve our identity in Him.

Humility

Our identity was never meant to be about us but about us being an image bearer of the glory of God, that others might come to know God.

Grace

Our identity comes by God's grace alone. We could never earn this identity and we cannot lose it, either.

Let's Recap

Shame is so insidious it defines us to the point that we forget who we are. It robs us of our true identity and steals the joy we can have by living free of shame. Some of the ways we lose our God-given identity include shame caused by failure to perform; pretending or rationalizing away the shame; brokenness due to taking on the shame caused by someone close to us; and life changes that disorient and distract us. But even when we're lost or hiding, our God-given identity is waiting, dormant—our identity can be restored again! When we stand up to shame and recognize that our identity is in Christ, we learn to substitute acceptance for rejection; we learn that we are chosen, celebrated, and loved. We give up worrying about unpopularity, perfectionism, and insecurity. In fact, we are complete.

Reflection Questions

1. Have you ever let your former identity bring shame into your life?
2. What stumbling blocks keep you buried in shame?
3. What does it mean to you to have Christ's identity?

Name Your Shame—and Let It Go

DEVOTIONAL

Shame Off Our Performance

You must have the same attitude that
Christ Jesus had.
  Though he was God,
    he did not think of equality with God
    as something to cling to.
  Instead, he gave up his divine privileges;
    he took the humble position of a slave
    and was born as a human being.
  When he appeared in human form,
    he humbled himself in obedience to God
    and died a criminal's death on a cross.
                              —Philippians 2:5-8

Our performance does not define us. Our worth does not come from our performance. Some of you type-A people out there are nodding yes, but your mind is still driving you to think that you can just keep trying harder. (Not that I would know anything about that personality type).

What is it about a messed-up performance that shames us? We feel naked in front of others. We feel that our performance is tied to our identity, and in our humanness, we are uncomfortable with admitting that we are not perfect.

But every aspect of our performance is a gift from God who equips, calls, and gifts us to do what He has placed on our hearts.

Even though we can never be perfect, we strive for excellence not for our glory, but for God's. Any achievement we have we lay at His feet in gratitude. When we fall short of our performance goals, it's OK. We gave it our best.

A Prayer

Lord, thank You for the abilities You give. Remove shame off of us when we don't achieve what we hoped to and help us to be content with our best effort.

CHAPTER ELEVEN

Defeating Shame

Living in the Shame-Off-You Life

> *But we have renounced the hidden things of shame, not walking in craftiness, nor falsifying the word of God, but by manifestation of the truth, commending ourselves to every man's conscience before God.* —2 Corinthians 4:2 (BLB)

> Hidden things have a way of becoming found. Ready or not. —*Denise*

Shame cannot really be hidden. It can only be quieted for a while, while we try to call it by another name. And hidden things have a way of becoming found. Ready or not.

I wasn't ready for hidden things in my former husband's background to surface when they did. But I would not have wanted to be kept in the dark either. Not for one more second. There is no fitting language for the agony of the soul when a bomb goes off in your home and you try to grasp your new reality. It does not make sense. You can't accept it. The pieces do not add up. Until one by one the pieces begin to fit, and the horror grips your soul so tightly you struggle to breathe and exist, even function in the daily demands of life.

All I once thought I knew, I didn't. The background of the man I had married was a lie. The secrets of past sins were shielded from me to "protect" me. Funny, I did not feel so protected. I felt that my ex-husband was protected, while my children and I were exposed and vulnerable. One by one, stories were shared of experiences that happened long before I ever met him; those past ghosts were hidden only to resurface with new victims.

All the pieces of our lives shattered on the floor; the sting of betrayal bathed us in shame. How did I not know? How could he do that to our precious children? to me? Somehow within me I knew something wasn't right. I remembered times long ago when I had asked honest questions. The answers had all been lies. The truth had been hidden from me on purpose. And now shame was asking me to hide it in my life, too. Anything to avoid its stigma and the identity of being what I was: the wife of a sex offender. I wasn't to blame for his actions, I had done everything I could to protect my children, but the shame engulfed us nonetheless. We were one of them. Those families that were blown apart by hidden sin, and not just any sin—sexual sin. I could not say the words *sexual abuse* at first. The words hurt too much. And people tried to minimize the damage that my children and I suffered by analyzing the definition of *abuse*. The damage that was done to our souls by such indifferent and erroneous characterization only increased our shame. What classification were we? Broken. Violated. My children have struggled since then

Shame loses its power when we don't regard it.

to recover their worth. And they are recovering, by the grace and compassion of our living God.

Once for All Mankind

If anyone knew what it was to be shamed in public, it was Jesus' mother. A virtuous young woman of honor, she was innocent and wholesome. She felt no guilt. Caressing her growing belly, Mary knew there was no way to conceal what grew within her. Should she feel shame for this miracle of life? Shame for being the one to bear God Incarnate? Have you ever wondered why God would have her walk through such scorn from man when she was innocent? Why didn't the angel reveal God's plan to everyone to spare Mary the shame?

Mary's response is beautiful. There, in the midst of what was a potentially scandalous situation, she praises the Lord. She is obedient and does not complain about the shame people put upon her. She was looking to something beyond the here and now:

> And Mary said, "My soul exalts the Lord, and my spirit has begun to rejoice in God my Savior, because he has looked upon the humble state of his servant. For from now on all generations will call me blessed, because he who is mighty has done great things for me, and holy is his name; from generation to generation he is merciful to those who fear him. He has demonstrated power with his arm; he has scattered those whose pride wells up from the sheer arrogance of their hearts." (Luke 1:46-51 NET)

Being humbled is painful to our flesh. We don't like to die to self. But Mary recognized that her humbling was for an ultimate good far beyond the temporary scorn. Sometimes it might look like God does not care about the suffering that shame produces in our lives, but His purposes are always greater. And He chose the walk of shame, as well, though not for His own sins—for ours.

> When we help turn one sinner back toward God rather than shaming them further, we take the shame they are feeling and redeem it for good purposes.

Why would the Savior of the world be born in such humble circumstances? Shame did not rule Him, nor did man's opinion. We feel shame so deeply. We cannot understand why God wouldn't save the world without enduring shame since He has the power to do so. But God chose for His Son to go through the most shameful death of all on the cross. God chose for Jesus to be spat upon by the ones He made and to endure shame upon shame as Jesus carried His own cross. Jesus bore shame from the governing authorities, shame from the public, shame from criminals, shame from the church and its leaders, and shame from friends (Matthew 27:36-44). Was Jesus trying to show us a truth about shame even as He walked the road to Calvary? Shame loses its power when we don't regard it. When God chose for Jesus to die such a shameful death, He was removing the sting of death and shame.

This is hard for us to understand. We think avoiding shame would have been the best route. But by walking through the shame and all its scorn, our Lord showed us that He overcame. The shame this world places on us is temporary and placed on us by ourselves or by man. We have given shame too much power and allowed it to dominate us. Christ showed us the way. Walk through the shame rather than avoiding it. In the end, our Savior took all of our shame upon Himself by choosing to fulfill the offerings of His righteous law for His people. "For God made Christ, who never sinned, to be the offering for our sin, so that we could be made right with God through Christ" (2 Corinthians 5:21). Christ became the sacrificial Lamb, a sin offering, our guilt offering, setting us free from guilt and shame. Mary bore shame by becoming pregnant as a virgin and bearing the King of kings, who would choose to bear all of our shame. And He did it with joy. God's highest motivation was not the limiting of our shame, but the radical removal of it by facing it and being a sin offering for all—once for all mankind.

As Christ Did for Us

In Christ, even when we have shame in our lives, it is in acknowledging it that we find freedom from it. Shame is best defeated when we acknowledge it and address it biblically and lovingly. Humbling ourselves causes shame to lose its power. Shame cannot break through the armor of God that covers us. When we own it, we don't have to go around feeling guilty. Instead, we can be set free from shame because we saw our need of redemption.

And we can be Christ for others through our own example. By pointing them to a higher purpose and goal instead of remaining in their shame, we do the same thing that Christ did for us. Shame and suffering have a way of sobering us up to reality and what really matters—compassion for others, for example, and gratitude for the forgiveness and healing God brings even through shame. Growth in our character and in our relationship with God. Meanwhile, giving grace to others helps to set us and them free from shame's clutches and puts us on the cycle of Shame Off You instead.

The Work of a Lifetime

Maybe you understand the idea of redemption but still feel trapped in your shame. You feel defined by it as you try to grapple with removing it from your life. The voices of other people's accusations ring in your head while you try to silence them with God's voice. Give yourself grace. It might take a while to learn how to operate and function in this life without shame. And shame will arise again from time to time, needing to be processed biblically with truth, humility, and grace. Shame creates a host of dysfunctional behaviors in us and adopting a new mind-set takes time and practice. Replacing the negative dysfunction that shame produces takes honesty, vulnerability, and intentionality to be able to debunk shame. We need to examine our thoughts and evaluate them through the biblical lens to keep us living the shame-free life.

Bottom line? Defeating shame is not a once-and-done proposition. Learning to hear the voice of God and follow it takes some practice. It is part of the growth curve. There is no shame in that either. Punishing ourselves by holding on to shame is not God's plan for us. Forgiveness is. But we have to choose to accept and walk in that forgiveness. Every single day. Nothing separates us from God's love and freedom but ourselves.

When we feel shame creeping into our lives, whether it be from our own transgression or not, we have to be discerning and vigilant. God stands ready to help restore us to who we are in Christ.

And the work of God is beautiful. Those who were once bound in fear become free once again. Those crushed with insecurity stand secure in Christ. Those who were self-conscious are restored to a healthy confidence. The rejected are now accepted. The anxious are now peaceful. Those who were absorbed in self and self-focused are now others-centered, useful to help others become shame-free. The needy are now fulfilled. Those who were paranoid are now able to trust again. The depressed become hopeful and the inferior are esteemed.

I never would have chosen the path to get to where I am today, yet God used it all to heal and restore me. The shame I felt at the revelation of sin in our life, in the courtroom, and in the public eye has been overcome by God's Word and His Spirit. I had to learn to recognize shame in order to be able to let go of it. Frankly, we are never fully done with shame in this fallen world. That's OK, though, because now we know how to rid ourselves of it using the biblical lens.

So use the strategies we've discussed here, friends. Believe in God. Read the Word. Forgive yourself and others. Be generous and compassionate, as God is with us. Feel gratitude. Dispense grace. Let go of guilt. Hold to hope in Christ. Abide in Him.

An Inner Circle

Who gets to be in your inner circle? A lot of the shame we encounter in this life comes in the relationships we have with the people in our inner circle. We have to expose dysfunctional patterns to be able to heal. As we seek to do so in a godly manner, the Lord restores what is broken. New habits are hard, but when we are diligent to extinguish shame—not through pride or simply by dismissing it, but by honestly assessing shame through truth, grace, and humility—we are set free. Shame-free.

It took many years to heal from the layers of shame that encompassed me, but the joy that fills my soul is unparalleled from any time in my life. If shame arises now, I know what to do with it. And what the locusts have eaten, God has restored. Shame off me. And now it's your turn, friend: Shame Off You.

God's Restoration Comes Full Circle

God has promises in His Word that we can count on. Even when it seems as if the locusts have devoured any hope of restoration. As we press in to trust in His promises and bathe our minds in His Word, God heals us. And sometimes He even blesses us abundantly.

Like Ruth who ventured to a new land before she would meet Boaz, I had to leave what I knew and go to a new place, too. That invitation ended up changing my life. That altar I wept upon the first Sunday at the new church? I wept there again and again as the Lord healed me from the stifling shame and grief. One time in particular God used a human to comfort me. The man who had compassion on me as I wept once again? You met him earlier. I call him my "Bo"— that's short for Boaz—and I am blessed to be married to him. God used him to redeem my life and bring healing that I never thought was possible. Sometimes God removes our shame by His presence and His Word. And sometimes He also lovingly brings people into our lives to comfort us when we need it most. What the locusts ate, my God has restored. Faithful God. Shame Off Me.

Review and Reflection

Truth

Recognizing that we have adapted to a culture of shame helps to set us free from it. We have a role to play, too. Letting go of trying to please others and a dysfunctional response of enabling others, we pave the way to healthier relationships. We are not trapped and can choose to respond to shame biblically.

Humility

Perhaps we have been toxic ourselves. Maybe we recognize the tactics of toxic people because we have used those tactics ourselves. We might need to let go of trying to control others and adopt healthier communication patterns. The best defense is to go on the offense and pray for the shame violators in our lives. Then we can pray that we will not participate in that behavior, too.

Grace

When people shame us, they most likely are not even aware of their dysfunction themselves. Praying for them and addressing the shame in humility help us extend the grace we need, ourselves.

Prayer

God, help me to see hidden shame in my life and to run to you to remove all the shame I encounter. Keep me from being deceived by sin and shame and help me to cultivate healthy relationships in my life that produce honor and glorify You.

Let's Recap

Our loving God chose to walk through shame to bring us salvation. Avoiding shame will not produce the victorious life God has for us, but processing shame biblically enables us to rise and walk through shame just like our Savior did. When we detect people in our inner circle who shame us, we are not stuck in that situation. God has empowered us to walk through the door of shame with truth, humility, and grace so we can stay off the cycle of shame and avoid the condemnation that shame brings. We will encounter shame in this fallen world, but shame loses its power when we do not become entrapped by it.

Reflection Questions

1. Spend some quiet time reflecting on the shame you've identified in yourself. Have you been able to let some of it go? In what areas do you still need work?

2. Shame Off You is not a once-and-done proposition. It requires vigilance and self-examination. Do you have a maintenance plan for this?

3. Remember grace. Show it to others—and remember to give yourself grace, too. You're only human.

Name Your Shame—and Let It Go

DEVOTIONAL

Living the Shame-Off-You Life

Make no friendship with a man given to anger, nor go with a wrathful man, lest you learn his ways and entangle yourself in a snare. —Proverbs 22:24-25 (ESV)

Here we are at the end of our exploration of shame. How have you recognized shame in your life? What's that? Ashamed to talk about it? No, not you! Not anymore. Because shame does not have a hold on you or define you any longer.

Living this Shame-Off-You life will take having the right people in our lives, so Proverbs seems a fitting place to end our journey. Recognizing the toxicity of shame in our relationships helps us to defuse it and put boundaries in place to keep the shame out. It is by living a Christ-centered life based upon the truth of His word that we will tame the shame in our lives. While shame can be formed within our own hearts, shame placed on us by other people is rife in our culture. Recognizing that we have adapted to a culture of shame helps to set us free from it. We have a role to play, too. We are not trapped and can choose to respond to shame biblically—with truth, humility, and grace.

Prayer

God, help me to see hidden shame in my life and to run to you to remove all the shame I encounter. Keep me from being deceived by sin and shame and help me to cultivate healthy relationships in my life that produce honor and glorify You.

Scriptures to Remove

Shame Off You

A Reference Guide

Scripture Credits

This page lists the Scripture credits for those translations appearing in the reference guide. It does not include the credits already given on the copyright page.

Scripture quotations taken from the Amplified® Bible (AMP), Copyright © 2015 by The Lockman Foundation. Used by permission. www.Lockman.org

Scripture quotations marked BSB are taken from The Holy Bible, Berean Study Bible, BSB Copyright © 2016, 2018 by Bible Hub. Used by Permission. All Rights Reserved Worldwide.

Scripture quotations noted CEB are taken from the Common English Bible, copyright 2011. Used by permission. All rights reserved.

Scripture quotations marked (CEV) are from the Contemporary English Version Copyright © 1991, 1992, 1995 by American Bible Society. Used by Permission.

Scripture quotations marked KJV are from The Authorized (King James) Version. Rights in the Authorized Version in the United Kingdom are vested in the Crown. Reproduced by permission of the Crown's patentee, Cambridge University Press.

Scripture marked NCV is taken from the New Century Version®. Copyright © 2005 by Thomas Nelson. Used by permission. All rights reserved.

Scripture marked NHEB is taken from the New Heart English Bible and is in the public domain.

Scripture taken from the New King James Version®. Copyright © 1982 by Thomas Nelson. Used by permission. All rights reserved.

Dear Reader,

First, I want to thank you for joining the Shame Off You movement. My heartfelt prayer is that this book will change your life and set you free from shame's shackles so you can help set others free, too.

As Shame Off You reveals a biblical process to remove shame from our lives and replace it with the abundant, joyful life Christ promises us, I want to equip you further with Scriptures specific to shame. I hope this collection will do just that as an accompaniment guide.

The word of God is our greatest asset in our hunt for freedom from shame. Use this guide to examine shame in your life. Each topic of shame listed here will have three Scripture references exploring:

- The root of shame (underlying cause of the shame being exhibited)
- The fruit of shame (what the shame is doing in your life)
- The cure for shame (a way out of the particular cycle of shame you are experiencing)

Once we discover the root and fruit of shame, we can determine the best route out of shame through God's word and find the cure He supplies.

To further help you overcome shame, there is a section with Scriptures to help you defeat shame, followed by a section of promises from God's Word for us.

Don't be put off by shame—when we are willing to look at shame and see the truth with humility and grace, we can overcome it. Shame is not a life sentence for those who are willing to examine it and walk in God's liberating truth.

I will be in prayer for you as you continue on your quest to be shame free. Come and visit with me at www.shameoffyou.life or in the Shame Off You group where community happens: www .facebook.com/groups/shameoffyou. I'll see you there!

Shame Off You, friend!

Topics of Shame

Age

Why do we feel shame for our age, especially when the Bible says it is a blessing and an honor to have lived long? Every age we encounter has lessons to learn, and there is no shame in that.

Shame's Root: Shame from our age is rooted in feeling useless.
> "Do not cast me off in the time of old age; forsake me not when my strength is spent." (Psalm 71:9 ESV)

Shame's Fruit: Discouragement arises when we feel shame for our age, but our Spirit can be renewed.
> "So we do not lose heart. Though our outer self is wasting away, our inner self is being renewed day by day." (2 Corinthians 4:16 ESV)

Shame's Cure: Recognize and believe God's truth and promises about age over man's opinions.
> "Gray hair is a crown of glory; it is gained in a righteous life." (Proverbs 16:31 ESV)

Anger

Anger can stem from a lack of self-control that can often exhibit passionate behavior that does not glorify God. We feel shame in our anger and when others are angry with us.

Shame's Root: Folly is at the root of anger.
> "Fools vent their anger, but the wise quietly hold it back." (Proverbs 29:11)

Shame's Fruit: Anger leads us away from righteousness.
> "For human anger does not accomplish God's righteousness." (James 1:20 NET)

Shame's Cure: Seeing God as our righteousness helps us discard shame at being angry with Him.
> "They will say of Me, 'Only in the Lord are righteousness

and strength.' Men will come to Him, and all who were angry at Him will be put to shame." (Isaiah 45:24 NASB)

Anxiety

Life is hard. Really hard. Our Savior admitted that truth, too, and even experienced anxiety in the Garden of Gethsemane. Why should we feel shame when anxiety visits us? Instead, we can bring out anxiety to God and extinguish it with the peace Christ offers us.

Shame's Root: Our hearts are anxious when we focus on our problems instead of our great God.

"Peace I leave with you; my peace I give to you. Not as the world gives do I give to you. Let not your hearts be troubled, neither let them be afraid." (John 14:27 ESV)

Shame's Fruit: Anxiety is our choice—to let our hearts be anxious or believe in God.

"Do not let your hearts be troubled. You believe in God; believe also in me." (John 14:1 NIV)

Shame's Cure: Admitting and surrendering our anxiety to the Lord removes its shame.

"[Cast] all your anxieties on him, because he cares for you." (1 Peter 5:7 ESV)

Appearance

Comparison is at the root of shame that we experience from appearance. Our looks, weight, fashion could never define our worth.

Shame's Root: Man looks at our exterior, but God looks at our heart.

"But the LORD said to Samuel, 'Do not consider his appearance or his height, for I have rejected him. The LORD does not look at the things people look at. People look at the outward appearance, but the LORD looks at the heart.'" (1 Samuel 16:7 NIV)

Shame's Fruit: Shame comes from making excuses and trying to justify ourselves to put on a show.

"He said to them, 'You are the ones who justify yourselves in the eyes of others, but God knows your hearts. What people value highly is detestable in God's sight.'" (Luke 16:15 NIV)

Shame's Cure: Judge by God's truth, not our own perspective.

"Do not judge according to external appearance, but judge with proper judgment." (John 7:24 NET)

Bad Company

Who we hang with is important. Christ hung out with sinners. We need to surround ourselves with people who point us to Christ, but we need not feel shame for being in the company of people who are not esteemed.

Shame's Root: Those we hang out with could cause us to reap shame if they do not walk with God.

"Do not be deceived: God cannot be mocked. A man reaps what he sows." (Galatians 6:7 NIV)

Shame's Fruit: We can get deceived by poor company.

"Do not be deceived: 'Bad company corrupts good morals.'" (1 Corinthians 15:33 NET)

Shame's Cure: Walk with wise people who fear God.

"The one who associates with the wise grows wise, but a companion of fools suffers harm." (Proverbs 13:20 NET)

Betrayal

When others have betrayed us, we can feel as if something is wrong with us. Why could they not have been faithful? But betrayal is more an indication of the betrayer's weakness than our own. Shame off us!

Shame's Root: Foes can heap shame on us because we idolize the relationship.

"If an enemy were insulting me, I could endure it; if a foe were rising against me, I could hide. But, it is you, a man like myself, my companion, my close friend." (Psalm 55:12-13 NIV)

Shame's Fruit: Betrayal can cause us to feel shame and to retaliate, but God has our back.

"When they hurled their insults at him, he did not retaliate;

when he suffered, he made no threats. Instead, he entrusted himself to him who judges justly." (1 Peter 2:23 NIV)

Shame's Cure: Don't trust in man—trust in God.

"Put no trust in a neighbor; have no confidence in a friend; guard the doors of your mouth from her who lies in your arms; for the son treats the father with contempt, the daughter rises up against her mother, the daughter-in-law against her mother-in-law; a man's enemies are the men of his own house. But as for me, I will look to the LORD; I will wait for the God of my salvation; my God will hear me." (Micah 7:5-7 ESV)

Bitterness

It is hard to be better and not bitter when people hurt us, but bitterness hurts us more. There is no shame when we struggle with bitterness. Just shame if we stay there. Let it go.

Shame's Root: When we give in to bitterness instead of to God's grace, we feel shame.

"See to it that no one fails to obtain the grace of God; that no 'root of bitterness' springs up and causes trouble, and by it many become defiled." (Hebrews 12:15 ESV)

Shame's Fruit: Wisdom helps us rise above bitterness and not be bound by it or its shame.

"A person's wisdom yields patience; it is to one's glory to overlook an offense." (Proverbs 19:11 NIV)

Shame's Cure: Walk in the spirit, not the flesh.

"Get rid of all bitterness, rage, anger, harsh words, and slander, as well as all types of evil behavior. Instead, be kind to each other, tenderhearted, forgiving one another, just as God through Christ has forgiven you." (Ephesians 4:31-32)

Comparison

Insecurities and a lack of worth stem from comparison to others. But our worth never comes from putting down others or feeling as if we have to be like them. Our worth is not about us either. We were uniquely made to express the love of God to a lost world and our worth comes from Christ alone.

Shame's Root: Conceit is at the root of the shame we feel when we compare to others and fall short.

> "Do nothing from selfish ambition or conceit, but in humility count others more significant than yourselves." (Philippians 2:3 ESV)

Shame's Fruit: Comparison with others does not lead to true understanding.

> "Not that we dare to classify or compare ourselves with some of those who are commending themselves. But when they measure themselves by one another and compare themselves with one another, they are without understanding." (2 Corinthians 10:12 ESV)

Shame's Cure: What man esteems God does not.

> "But God chose the foolish things of the world to shame the wise; God chose the weak things of the world to shame the strong." (1 Corinthians 1:27 NIV)

Condemnation

When others put us down, we feel less than and unable to get out of the box of their perception of us. But in Christ, no condemnation remains. No shame can overcome the sacrifice of Christ on our behalf.

Shame's Root: Condemnation is shame, often stemming from ourselves.

> "Beloved, if our heart does not condemn us, we have confidence before God." (1 John 3:21 ESV)

Shame's Fruit: Condemnation is quelled when we believe.

> "Whoever believes in him is not condemned, but whoever does not believe is condemned already, because he has not believed in the name of the only Son of God." (John 3:18 ESV)

Shame's Cure: Accept the identity we have in Christ.

> "Therefore, there is now no condemnation for those who are in Christ Jesus." (Romans 8:1 NIV)

Deceit

When people lie to us or we participate in that behavior, shame is there to chide us. We were either too dumb to recognize the falsehood from another or feel shame for being dishonest ourselves. There is no one good (Romans 3:23), so deception is man's attempt to cover their shame. When we speak the truth to our souls, we let go of deception and the shame it brings and cling to Christ's mercy, instead.

Shame's Root: We need to renounce deceit to be free from its shame.
"Rather, we have renounced secret and shameful ways; we do not use deception, nor do we distort the word of God. On the contrary, by setting forth the truth plainly we commend ourselves to everyone's conscience in the sight of God." (2 Corinthians 4:2 NIV)

Shame's Fruit: Lies bind us and blind us so we cannot see.
"Then you will know the truth, and the truth will set you free." (John 8:32 NIV)

Shame's Cure: Speaking the truth in love helps us get on the correct path again.
"We will not be influenced by every new teaching we hear from people who are trying to fool us. They make plans and try any kind of trick to fool people into following the wrong path. No! Speaking the truth with love, we will grow up in every way into Christ, who is the head." (Ephesians 4:14-15 NCV)

Depression

Disillusionment and depression slip in unnoticed, sometimes, and we can feel guilt and condemnation that we are not able to be cheerful. Life can be disappointing, but when we bring our depression to Christ, He is able to change our perspective and help us find joy in Him.

Shame's Root: Helplessness
"Don't give up and be helpless in times of trouble." (Proverbs 24:10 CEV)

Shame's Fruit: Shame from depression leads to weariness.

"Consider him who endured such opposition from sinners, so that you will not grow weary and lose heart." (Hebrews 12:3 NIV)

Shame's Cure: Hoping in God delivers us from shame and depression.

"Why am I discouraged? Why is my heart so sad? I will put my hope in God! I will praise him again—my Savior and my God! (Psalm 43:5)

Disobedience

We experience shame when we disobey God. Sin has consequences that are intended to help us see our sin and shame so we will return to God.

Shame's Root: Unbelief.

"Such people claim they know God, but they deny him by the way they live. They are detestable and disobedient, worthless for doing anything good." (Titus 1:16)

Shame's Fruit: Isolation and a hardened heart.

"If anyone does not obey our instruction in this letter, take special note of that person and do not associate with him, so that he will be put to shame." (2 Thessalonians 3:14 NASB)

Shame's Cure: Obeying God's Word.

"I hold fast to your rules. O LORD, do not let me be ashamed!" (Psalm 119:31 NET)

Displaced Shame

Uh oh. Someone cast shame your direction, maybe even boldly to your face or behind your back. Once we have examined the shame to see if there is any merit, we can be free. And if there is merit? We are still free. Christ alone is our righteousness, and He does not condemn us.

Shame's Root: Focus on self

"Consider him who endured such opposition from sinners, so that you will not grow weary and lose heart." (Hebrews 12:3 NIV)

Shame's Fruit: Pressure

"If you fail under pressure, your strength is too small." (Proverbs 24:10)

Shame's Cure: Trust God and don't give in to fear.

"Do not lose heart or be afraid when rumors are heard in the land; one rumor comes this year, another the next, rumors of violence in the land and of ruler against ruler." (Jeremiah 51:46 NIV)

Enemies

Enemies can cause us to feel insecure and less than. But when we trust in God, we don't have to receive their shame.

Shame's Root: Fear

"Do not be afraid of them; the Lord your God himself will fight for you." (Deuteronomy 3:22 NIV)

Shame's Fruit: Lack of trusting God

"I trust in you; do not let me be put to shame, nor let my enemies triumph over me." (Psalm 25:2 NIV)

Shame's Cure: Trusting in God's deliverance

"The Lord will fight for you; you need only to be still." (Exodus 14:14 NIV)

Failure

You messed up. OK. We all do. Ask God for forgiveness and look for the real root problem. Give yourself grace. Christ did.

Shame's Root: Putting confidence in our flesh

"My flesh and my heart may fail, but God is the strength of my heart and my portion forever." (Psalm 73:26 ESV)

Shame's Fruit: Falling repetitively

"The righteous may fall seven times but still get up, but the wicked will stumble into trouble." (Proverbs 24:16 CEB)

Shame's Cure: Trusting in God to complete the work in us

"And I am certain that God, who began the good work

within you, will continue his work until it is finally finished on the day when Christ Jesus returns." (Philippians 1:6)

False Shame

Sometimes we can feel shame for something that is not even shameful. We can't explain it, but we feel like we should do more. If there's no proof, tell your soul the truth. Shame Off You!

Shame's Root: Pride and false humility
>"Every way of a man is right in his own eyes, but the Lord weighs the heart." (Proverbs 21:2 ESV)

Shame's Fruit: Attempting to establish worth by condemning others with the condemnation we received.
>"Therefore, you have no excuse, O man, every one of you who judges. For in passing judgment on another you condemn yourself, because you, the judge, practice the very same things." (Romans 2:1 ESV)

Shame's Cure: God is powerful and able to help us think rightly and overcome judgment.
>"For God hath not given us the spirit of fear; but of power, and of love, and of a sound mind." (2 Timothy 1:7 KJV)

Fear

When we feel afraid, we sometimes also feel shame. We should trust God. But God wants to comfort us in our fear, not shame us because of it.

Shame's Root: Trust issues
>"Do not be afraid or discouraged, for the LORD will personally go ahead of you. He will be with you; he will neither fail you nor abandon you." (Deuteronomy 31:8)

Shame's Fruit: Insecurity—not walking in love
>"Such love has no fear, because perfect love expels all fear. If we are afraid, it is for fear of punishment, and this shows that we have not fully experienced his perfect love." (1 John 4:18)

Shame's Cure: God's promises are greater than any fear we feel. "Do not be afraid; you will not be put to shame. Do not fear disgrace; you will not be humiliated. You will forget the shame of your youth and remember no more the reproach of your widowhood." (Isaiah 54:4 NIV)

Finances

Not having enough or having too much can both cause shame. But when we consider that it all belongs to God anyway, we are just grateful stewards of His provision. Finances don't give us value; Christ does.

Shame's Root: Trying to win acceptance through belongings
"The poor are shunned by all their relatives—how much more do their friends avoid them! Though the poor pursue them with pleading, they are nowhere to be found." (Proverbs 19:7 NIV)

Shame's Fruit: Greed blinds us from what matters most.
"Otherwise, I may have too much and disown you and say, 'Who is the LORD?' Or I may become poor and steal, and so dishonor the name of my God." (Proverbs 30:9 NIV)

Shame's Cure: Remember that everything comes from God.
"But remember the LORD your God, for it is he who gives you the ability to produce wealth, and so confirms his covenant, which he swore to your ancestors, as it is today." (Deuteronomy 8:18 NIV)

Fornication or Adultery

Whether we have been the recipient of another person's unfaithfulness or fallen short ourselves, shame knocks on the door of our hearts and minds. The scarlet letter feels like a permanent label, but there is healing when we bring our sin and shame to Christ and ask Him to cover us in His righteousness.

Shame's Root: Forgetting we house the Holy Spirit in jars of clay
"Do you not know that your bodies are temples of the Holy Spirit, who is in you, whom you have received from God?

You are not your own; you were bought at a price. Therefore honor God with your bodies." (1 Corinthians 6:19-20 NIV)

Shame's Fruit: Suffering for poor choices

"Blows and disgrace are his lot, and his shame will never be wiped away." (Proverbs 6:33 NIV)

Shame's Cure: Choosing faithfulness over flesh

"Let love and faithfulness never leave you; bind them around your neck, write them on the tablet of your heart. Then you will win favor and a good name in the sight of God and man." (Proverbs 3:3-4 NIV)

Forsaking God

The Bible says that no one who seeks God is perfect, except by His grace. When we fall short, we don't have to hide. Run to Him. He is waiting.

Shame's Root: Not acknowledging God

"The gracious hand of our God is on everyone who looks to him, but his great anger is against all who forsake him." (Ezra 8:22 NIV)

Shame's Fruit: Living apart from God

"O LORD, the hope of Israel, All who forsake You will be put to shame. Those who turn away on earth will be written down, Because they have forsaken the fountain of living water, even the LORD." (Jeremiah 17:13 NASB)

Shame's Cure: Choosing to fear and serve God.

"Then the people answered, 'Far be it from us to forsake the LORD to serve other gods!'" (Joshua 24:16 NIV)

Gluttony

Craving outside of God's blessing in excess will bring us shame. Why? Because we will likely bear fruit for this craving and the behavior of gluttony is "piggish."

Shame's Root: Craving

"It's not good to eat too much honey, and it's not good to seek honors for yourself." (Proverbs 25:27)

Shame's Fruit: Enslaved to what we want

"Young people who obey the law are wise; those with wild friends bring shame to their parents." (Proverbs 28:7)

Shame's Cure: Being set free through Christ

"You say, 'I am allowed to do anything'—but not everything is good for you. And even though 'I am allowed to do anything,' I must not become a slave to anything." (1 Corinthians 6:12)

Gossip/Slander

So and so said something about you, or maybe you said it about them. Like other sins, we have to recognize our part in it and turn from it if we are guilty. When others talk about us, too, we have a choice to make: either become fixated on the gossip/slander or fix our minds on Christ's view of us, that we do not deserve.

Shame's Root: Fear of judgment or fear of man

"Blessed are you when people insult you, persecute you and falsely say all kinds of evil against you because of me." (Matthew 5:11 NIV)

Shame's Fruit: Tearing down others to justify self

"Argue your case with your neighbor himself, and do not reveal another's secret, lest he who hears you bring shame upon you, and your ill repute have no end." (Proverbs 25:9-10 ESV)

Shame's Cure: Praying and trusting God to defend us

"May the arrogant be ashamed, for they subvert me with a lie; But I shall meditate on Your precepts." (Psalm 119:78 NASB)

Health Issues

When we receive a diagnosis, we can feel shame. Others seem healthy; why do we have health issues? Living in a fallen world where we will all face death means illness could play a part. But each person has their own burdens to bear and maybe our health problems can become a testimony and a mission from God.

Shame's Root: Discouragement from health troubles

"Though you have made me see troubles, many and bitter, you will restore my life again; from the depths of the earth you will again bring me up. You will increase my honor and comfort me once more." (Psalm 71:20-21 NIV)

Shame's Fruit: Desperate for faith/belief that God can heal us

"And the prayer offered in faith will make the sick person well; the Lord will raise them up. If they have sinned, they will be forgiven. Therefore, confess your sins to each other and pray for each other so that you may be healed. The prayer of a righteous person is powerful and effective." (James 5:15-16 NIV)

Shame's Cure: God is our strength, whether or not we ever experience physical healing.

"The LORD sustains them on their sickbed and restores them from their bed of illness." (Psalm 41:3 NIV)

Hidden Shame

Shame is not always easily recognizable, but it can be creating havoc in our lives behind the scenes, nonetheless. It might happen when we rationalize away our shortcomings or consider it to just be a part of who we are or a part of our culture. Making excuses about shame won't dismiss it, though. When we ask God to reveal hidden sins or shames, He is faithful to set us free from them.

Shame's Root: Pride—not wanting to see our own sin and shame

"Whoever conceals their sins does not prosper, but the one who confesses and renounces them finds mercy." (Proverbs 28:13 NIV)

Shame's Fruit: Controlled by shame

"How can I know all the sins lurking in my heart? Cleanse me from these hidden faults. Keep your servant from deliberate sins! Don't let them control me. Then I will be free of guilt and innocent of great sin." (Psalm 19:12-13)

Shame's Cure: Cultivate an eternal perspective and expose things in the dark to be set free.

"Keep thinking about things above, not things on the earth, for you have died and your life is hidden with Christ in God." (Colossians 3:2-3 NET)

Humiliation

Humiliation makes us want to disappear. We feel like we cannot escape it; it is in our minds. But the root word of humiliation is beautiful: humility.

Shame's Root: Unfaithfulness

"Lord, you are righteous, but this day we are covered with shame . . . because of our unfaithfulness to you." (Daniel 9:7 (NIV)

Shame's Fruit: Overwhelmed

"All day long my dishonor is before me and my humiliation has overwhelmed me." (Psalm 44:15 NASB)

Shame's Cure: Confidence in God's grace, not our own strength.

"But he said to me, 'My grace is sufficient for you, for my power is made perfect in weakness.' Therefore I will boast all the more gladly about my weaknesses, so that Christ's power may rest on me." (2 Corinthians 12:9 NIV)

Idolatry

We might not be carving items and bowing down to worship our creation, but there are other things that our hearts can run after today. Where our chief time or money investment is can often reveal an idol in our midst.

Shame's Root: Worshipping things instead of God

"How foolish are those who manufacture idols. These prized objects are really worthless. The people who worship idols don't know this, so they are all put to shame." (Isaiah 44:9)

Shame's Fruit: Humiliation.

"They will be put to shame and even humiliated, all of

them; The manufacturers of idols will go away together in humiliation." (Isaiah 45:16 NASB)

Shame's Cure: Only worship God alone.

"You shall have no other gods before me. You shall not make for yourself an image in the form of anything in heaven above or on the earth beneath or in the waters below." (Exodus 20:3-4 NIV)

Insecurity

We can often feel shame for our personhood. We don't feel as if we are enough. God's thoughts about us say differently. He is crazy about us and does not define us by people's judgments. No one can affect His view of us!

Shame's Root: Feeling unloved can create a chasm of insecurity.

"And I pray that you, being rooted and established in love, may have power, together with all the Lord's holy people, to grasp how wide and long and high and deep is the love of Christ, and to know this love that surpasses knowledge— that you may be filled to the measure of all the fullness of God." (Ephesians 3:17-19 NIV)

Shame's Fruit: Recognize insecurity as worry and seek God in the midst.

"So do not worry, saying, 'What shall we eat?' or 'What shall we drink?' or 'What shall we wear?' For the pagans run after all these things, and your heavenly Father knows that you need them. But seek first his kingdom and his righteousness, and all these things will be given to you as well." (Matthew 6:31-33 NIV)

Shame's Cure: See our value in Christ and believe that instead of man's opinion.

"Many, O Lord my God, are Your wonderful works which You have done; And Your thoughts toward us cannot be recounted to You in order; if I would declare and speak of them, they are more than can be numbered." (Psalm 40:5 NKJV)

Jealousy

Jealousy can take the joy out of life. When we compare to others, we are missing the point. We were each created to be different, not the same. Jealousy is discontent with our status in this life. But God can help us adopt a kingdom mentality that roots others on and recognizes that other people's achievements does not cast a shadow on ours.

Shame's Root: Jealousy is often accompanied by other evil practices. "For where jealousy and selfish ambition exist, there will be disorder and every vile practice." (James 3:16 ESV)

Shame's Fruit: Jealousy is poisonous and harms us. "A peaceful heart leads to a healthy body; jealousy is like cancer in the bones." (Proverbs 14:30)

Shame's Cure: Put on love. Love wants the best for others, rather than being jealous of them. "Love is patient and kind. Love is not jealous or boastful or proud." (1 Corinthians 13:4)

Lack of Discipline

You bombed the diet again. Or failed to exercise. Maybe even forgot to do your devotions. No need for shame. God knew we needed a Savior and battling the flesh is a constant effort.

Shame's Root: Lack of discipline comes from our folly. "For lack of discipline they will die, led astray by their own great folly." (Proverbs 5:23 NIV)

Shame's Fruit: Lack of discipline can lead to poverty and shame. "Poverty and shame come to him who ignores discipline, but whoever heeds correction will be honored." (Proverbs 13:18 BSB)

Shame's Cure: The fruit of discipline is peace and righteousness. "For the moment all discipline seems painful rather than pleasant, but later it yields the peaceful fruit of righteousness to those who have been trained by it." (Hebrews 12:11 ESV)

Laziness

Some shame can be a motivator. Being lazy does not honor God, but sometimes we can feel like we are lazy when we are not. Maybe health challenges or other responsibilities prevent us from accomplishing what we intended to. Receive a rebuke if you need to (the Bible says it is oil on your head) or let go of false accusations. Maybe prioritize your work and see what you need to let go of.

Shame's Root: Laziness can demonstrate a lack of wisdom.
"He who gathers in summer is a son who acts wisely, but he who sleeps in harvest is a son who acts shamefully." (Proverbs 10:5 NASB)

Shame's Fruit: Being lazy leads to lack of growth.
"He becomes poor who works with a lazy hand, but the hand of the diligent brings wealth. He who gathers in summer is a wise son, but he who sleeps during the harvest is a son who causes shame." (Proverbs 10:4-5 NHEB)

Shame's Cure: Work hard for the glory of God. He will reward us!
"Work willingly at whatever you do, as though you were working for the Lord rather than for people. Remember that the Lord will give you an inheritance as your reward, and that the Master you are serving is Christ." (Colossians 3:23-24)

Minds

The battle for shame truly is in the mind. Other people might not even be shaming us at all, but we think they are. Or we shame ourselves all on our own. Bathing our mind in God's word helps us evaluate shame's validity through the lens of truth, humility, and grace.

Shame's Root: Our minds are naturally fleshly, against God.
"Because the carnal mind is enmity against God; for it is not subject to the law of God, nor indeed can be." (Romans 8:7 NKJV)

Shame's Fruit: What we fix our thoughts on we will become.
"And now, dear brothers and sisters, one final thing. Fix

your thoughts on what is true, and honorable, and right, and pure, and lovely, and admirable. Think about things that are excellent and worthy of praise." (Philippians 4:8)

Shame's Cure: Disciplining our minds and fixing our thoughts upon God's grace sets us free.

"Therefore, prepare your minds for action, keep sober in spirit, fix your hope completely on the grace to be brought to you at the revelation of Jesus Christ." (1 Peter 1:13 NASB)

Parenting (shame for parent)

Oh my. Your kid just did something to embarrass you. Wait . . . that's displaced shame. Still, we as parents can shame our kids or feel pride or shame for their successes or failures. Unless we apply God's principles. Ultimately, we do not own anyone else's shame. Ever.

Shame's Root: The root of shame in parenting comes from folly.
"Folly is bound up in the heart of a child." (Proverbs 22:15 NIV)

Shame's Fruit: Spoiling a child could bring parents shame.
"A child who gets his own way brings shame to his mother." (Proverbs 29:15 NASB)

Shame's Cure: When we love our children, we are careful to discipline them to free them from folly.
"Those who love their children care enough to discipline them." (Proverbs 13:24)

Peer pressure

If we don't measure up to someone else's expectations, we can feel the pressure (shame) to do so. That is only if we believe the lie that we have to. We can overcome shame from peer pressure by recognizing that the only standard we are to follow is Christ's.

Shame's Root: Who we choose to walk with will impact our life greatly.
"Walk with the wise and become wise, for a companion of fools suffers harm." (Proverbs 13:20 NIV)

Shame's Fruit: Following a crowd will not keep us safe from shame. "Behold, all his companions shall be put to shame, and the craftsmen are only human. Let them all assemble, let them stand forth. They shall be terrified; they shall be put to shame together." (Isaiah 44:11 ESV)

Shame's Cure: Emulate God's ways, not man's.

"Don't copy the behavior and customs of this world, but let God transform you into a new person by changing the way you think. Then you will learn to know God's will for you, which is good and pleasing and perfect." (Romans 12:2)

Persecution

When we embrace Christ and live for Him, we will not necessarily be wildly popular in a fallen world. When we cave to the fear of man and are ashamed of our faith, it results in shame.

Shame's Fruit: Don't shrink back when you are persecuted. There is no shame in following God.

"If anyone is ashamed of me and my words in this adulterous and sinful generation, the Son of Man will be ashamed of them when he comes in his Father's glory with the holy angels." (Mark 8:38 NIV)

Shame's Root: God's glory and not our own

"But it is no shame to suffer for being a Christian. Praise God for the privilege of being called by his name!" (1 Peter 4:16)

Shame's Cure: God has power to strengthen us when we are shamed for professing Christ.

"For I am not ashamed of the gospel, for it is the power of God for salvation to everyone who believes, to the Jew first and also to the Greek." (Romans 1:16 ESV)

Position

You did not place in a contest or get that position you really wanted. Ugh. You hope no one finds out. Why?! At least you tried. And maybe the position you did not achieve was not meant for you, anyway, but your willingness to participate in trying might be something that equips you for a position that you were meant for.

Shame's Root: Guilt tries to confine us in a position/state of shame.

> "If I am guilty, too bad for me; and even if I'm innocent, I can't hold my head high, because I am filled with shame and misery." (Job 10:15)

Shame's Fruit: Our positions in this life can be wrought by our sin and bring us shame.

> "After I strayed, I repented; after I came to understand, I beat my breast. I was ashamed and humiliated because I bore the disgrace of my youth." (Jeremiah 31:19 NIV)

Shame's Cure: God's purpose will prevail. Trust Him when our temporary positions bring shame.

> "And we know that in all things God works for the good of those who love him, who have been called according to his purpose." (Romans 8:28 NIV)

Presumptions

Assuming causes a lot of unnecessary grief and strife. When we presume upon another person motives they are supposedly having, that is pride. When others presume things of us, we are not accountable to their belief.

Shame's Root: Presumptions can run and ruin our lives.

> "Be careful what you think, because your thoughts run your life. Don't use your mouth to tell lies; don't ever say things that are not true. Keep your eyes focused on what is right, and look straight ahead to what is good. Be careful what you do, and always do what is right. Don't turn off the road of goodness; keep away from evil paths." (Proverbs 4:23-27 NCV)

Shame's Fruit: Presumption leads to strife.

> "Through pride and presumption come nothing but strife, but [skillful and godly] wisdom is with those who welcome [well-advised] counsel." (Proverbs 13:10 AMP)

Shame's Cure: Listen carefully rather than assuming.
"Spouting off before listening to the facts is both shameful and foolish." (Proverbs 18:13)

Pride

Shame's incubator is pride. Pride blinds us to shame's presence and tells us we are OK just as we are. A prescription of truth, grace, and humility will help us silence pride and gain honor.

Shame's Root: Pride will be our ruin.
"Too much pride will destroy you." (Proverbs 16:18 CEV)
Shame's Fruit: Pride breeds shame.
"Too much pride can put you to shame. It's wiser to be humble." (Proverbs 11:2 CEV)
Shame's Cure: Recognize that pride is against God. Destroy it and choose humility.
"We fight with weapons that are different from those the world uses. Our weapons have power from God that can destroy the enemy's strong places. We destroy people's arguments and every proud thing that raises itself against the knowledge of God. We capture every thought and make it give up and obey Christ." (2 Corinthians 10:4-5 NCV)

Quarrelsomeness

Fighting often leads to shame. We feel guilt for our part and consequently either shame others for having something we coveted or perhaps they do that to us. But striving and ambition cease when we cultivate a grateful heart and surrender our plans to God's.

Shame's Root: Our desires lead us down the path of shameful fighting.
"What causes fights and quarrels among you? Don't they come from your desires that battle within you?" (James 4:1 NIV)
Shame's Fruit: Recognize that the battle is spiritual. The flesh leads us to shame, the Spirit to honor.

"For those who live according to the flesh set their minds on the things of the flesh, but those who live according to the Spiritset their minds on the things of the Spirit. For to set the mind on the flesh is death, but to set the mind on the spirit is life and peace." (Romans 8:5-6 ESV)

Shame's Cure: Avoid strife and choose peace.

"It is to one's honor to avoid strife, but every fool is quick to quarrel." (Proverbs 20:3 NIV)

Rejection

You weren't invited to a gathering. Again. Or maybe people shun you. It is hard not to take rejection personally. But when we have been accepted by Christ, we no longer have to have acceptance from all. Maybe they are just not your tribe. Focusing on offering acceptance to other people who might need it helps us remove the focus from ourselves.

Shame's Root: Sometimes a history of rejection causes shame.

"Even if my father and mother abandon me, the LORD will hold me close." (Psalm 27:10)

Shame's Fruit: Shame crushes us if we let it. Jesus taught us how to disregard shame to walk in victory.

"We do this by keeping our eyes on Jesus, the champion who initiates and perfects our faith. Because of the joy awaiting him, he endured the cross, disregarding its shame. Now he is seated in the place of honor beside God's throne." (Hebrews 12:2)

Shame's Cure: Believing in God delivers us from shame.

"As you come to him, a living stone rejected by men but in the sight of God chosen and precious, you yourselves like living stones are being built up as a spiritual house, to be a holy priesthood, to offer spiritual sacrifices acceptable to God through Jesus Christ. For it stands in Scripture: 'Behold, I am laying in Zion a stone, a cornerstone chosen and precious, and whoever believes in him will not be put to shame.' " (1 Peter 2:4-6 ESV).

Sinning

When we fall short and sin, we can feel shame deeply. But we need not stay there. Praying and asking God to forgive us and to help us forgive ourselves can begin to rid us of shame.

Shame's Root: Ignorance can lead to shame and lead us to continue in sin.

"Come back to your senses as you ought, and stop sinning; for there are some who are ignorant of God—I say this to your shame." (1 Corinthians 15:34 NIV)

Shame's Fruit: Sinning separates us from God and covers us with guilt, but repentance restores us.

"And I said, 'O my God, I am ashamed and embarrassed to lift up my face to You, my God, for our iniquities have risen above our heads and our guilt has grown even to the heavens.'" (Ezra 9:6 NASB)

Shame's Cure: Seeking God and His righteousness turns us away from shame.

"Righteousness exalts a nation, but sin is a disgrace to any people." (Proverbs 14:34 NASB)

Suffering

Suffering is hard. We can feel ashamed that we are encountering suffering, as if something must be wrong with us. But suffering is common to man and no one gets to avoid it.

Shame's Root: Unmet expectations and encountering the unexpected.

"Dear friends, do not be surprised at the fiery ordeal that has come on you to test you, as though something strange were happening to you. But rejoice inasmuch as you participate in the sufferings of Christ, so that you may be overjoyed when his glory is revealed." (1 Peter 4:12-13 NIV)

Shame's Fruit: Disillusioned because of weakness.

"But he said to me, 'My grace is sufficient for you, for my power is made perfect in weakness.' Therefore, I will boast all the more gladly of my weaknesses, so that the power of Christ may rest upon me. For the sake of Christ, then, I am content with weaknesses, insults, hardships, persecutions, and calamities. For when I am weak, then I am strong." (2 Corinthians 12:9-10 ESV)

Shame's Cure: Asking God for His perspective and finding joy in identifying with His suffering.

"Looking to Jesus, the founder and perfecter of our faith, who for the joy that was set before him endured the cross, despising the shame, and is seated at the right hand of the throne of God." (Hebrews 12:2 ESV)

About the Author

Denise Pass is an award-winning CCM recording artist and singer-songwriter, accomplished writer/blogger, podcaster, and speaker and worship leader at women's conferences as well as a worship leader on staff at her home church. After the crushing discovery of her former husband's hidden life as a repetitive sex offender and survival of a painful divorce, she now shares an inspirational message through her ministry, Seeing Deep Ministries, about seeing the deeper truth in God's word when life hurts. Denise also founded and directed a home educational co-op for twelve years and engaged in many educational pursuits, including forming and directing a classical children's choir. A graduate of the University of Maryland, Denise now resides in Virginia with her kinsman-redeemer husband and five children. Find her online at DenisePass.com.